OVERCOME ANXIETY AND PANIC ATTACK

OVERCOME ANXIETY & PANIC ATTACK: RETRAIN YOUR ANXIOUS BRAIN, STOP DEPRESSION, FEAR, AND TOXIC RELATIONSHIP, REWIRE YOURSELF AND IMPROVE STRESS MANAGEMENT WITH (CBT) THERAPY WORKBOOK IN PLAIN ENGLISH.

Table of Contents

Introduction

Anxiety is a tough subject that, even when people seem to understand, they probably just do not. You'll hear "just calm down" and "get over it" more times than you can count. However, this isn't a great method for getting yourself back on track and back in control. People who repeat these age-old mantras to you are incredibly uneducated on the subject and they absolutely are not going to be helpful in moving forward in your treatment.

Luckily, with the help of this book, you'll be well on your way to taking control back from your fear and putting yourself back in the front seat of your behavior. There is hope, and there is a way to move forward even through the most trying of times. You aren't alone! You are surrounded by people who have dealt with the very same things in their lives and have a great handle on what needs to be done. Hope is always on the horizon.

There are absolutely ways to take the control back. It's hard, but it will not be for long. All things are manageable, all things shall pass. You might just need a little help in the meantime.

We'll tackle what anxiety is, how it comes to be in the first place, and why your brain seems so keen on working against you. There are so many factors which come into play when you are talking about anxiety, anyway! It really seems like a catchall that explains ever bit of fear or worry that might be plaguing your life daily. However, it's also a misnomer. Anxiety comes in many shapes and sizes- and those who deal with it need to wear many hats to cope!

The coping mechanisms that are so crucial to your development as a person and your ability to move forward in life are all in this book, waiting for you to uncover them. Different types of anxieties mean different coping mechanisms.

Chapter 1 Mindset

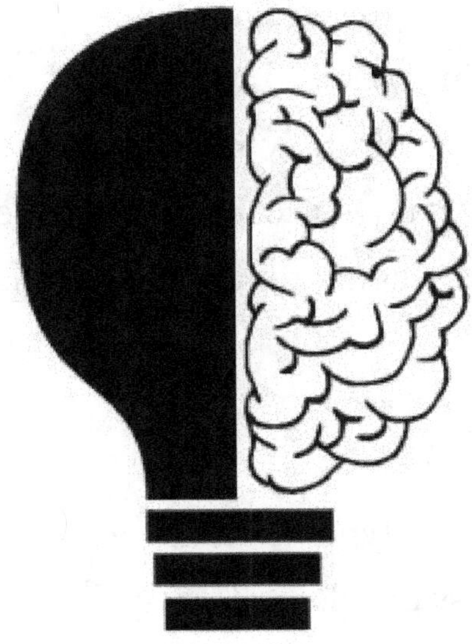

It might sound overwhelming at some point when an individual is told they are responsible for their own success in life. There are several studies that have been made on the complex organ known as the brain. These studies have been able to portray that an individual's beliefs play a very important role in what they are able to perceive as being able to achieve. These findings show the role mindset plays in steering an individual to achieving success in their life. Despite the presence of different forms and levels of success as perceived by people across the globe, there are generally accepted signs of success such as material wealth.

A person's mindset has a very simple and precise definition that can be universally applied. One can understand it as a set of assumptions or beliefs that are held by an individual person or group of people. Other definitions of this phenomenon consider a mindset as a person's or a group's views on life. As such, a mindset can become a powerful tool that influences the behavior and attitude of individuals around the world. And while mindsets tend to be culturally relevant, there is no doubt that there are universally accepted attitudes and beliefs. Consequently, we are going to take a closer look at them in the following sections.

Types of Mindsets

There are four major types of mindsets that are common in several people across the globe. They include:

1. Growth Mindset

This type of mindset is amazing for an individual to have in their life. There are unique qualities that are possessed by people who have a growth mindset. Such people are known to have strong desires and drive so as to grow themselves. This means that they constantly improve themselves day in day out. Such an individual loves to take different challenges in their daily life. The important aim of doing this is because they want to be better than they were yesterday.

It is very easy to spot an individual who has a growth mindset among other people. Such an individual is likely to go to the gym nearly every day. They are characterized by the attribute of loving to build their knowledge about themselves and the world in general. A good depiction of this mindset can be found in entrepreneurs and investors. Most of these people love to spot niches in the world and make the most out of them. They give several people employment as they continue to seek ways on how to generate more profit for themselves.

There are several advantages that people with a growth mindset possess. They are prone to improve in several areas of their life. The process of their growth is fast because they love challenges on a consistent basis. The other advantage of a person with a growth mindset is that they have a high success rate at work. It is because such an individual will aim to be better than the standard they had put on earlier. There are also demerits that come with an individual who has this kind of mindset. There are moments when such a person might be so focused on getting good results that they forget to actually enjoy their life.

    2. Fixed Mindset

The fixed mindset is characterized by being rather inflexible. Of course, this doesn't mean that it is a bad thing. What it means is that most individuals who have a fixed mindset are completely clear on what their values are and what they stand for. As such, they are confident in their abilities and will not waver easily. They are also open to change so long as it does not compromise their core values. This is the essence of the growth mindset. By being able to stay the course, even in the midst of a storm, folks with the fixed mindset can be sure that they are staying true to what they believe in.

It might sound overwhelming when an individual is told that their mindset has a big impact on their mental health. As such, embracing a fixed mindset can go a long way toward making sense of their thoughts and emotions. This entails knowing one's strengths and weakness in such a manner that one is able to make sense it. The fixed mindset can definitely prove to be very effective in achieving goals and objectives especially in the long run. However, the dark side of a fixed mindset can lead one to become overconfident and arrogant. An individual with this kind of character has the potential to destroy several meaningful relationships in their life.

3. Fear Mindset

There is a level of fear in every person regardless of their condition. It is a common characteristic among human beings to fear one thing or another. However, there are some people among us that let fear be there a major driving force behind their thoughts. Constant thoughts in an individual's mind have the potential of making them get stuck on a single issue. An individual with this kind of mindset has a low potential of bettering themselves. The major reason is always that fear tends to get the best of their abilities. So, instead of working on improving themselves, they may choose to "play it safe" and not go beyond their comfort zone.

There are several wonderful places an individual could go, or fantastic activities, one could participate in. However, the presence of a constant form of fear hinders such an individual from having these experiences. The common mentality among these people's minds is always avoiding certain life experiences to avoid or minimize risks. Such people are always underachievers in their lives. There are no advantages that come to an individual who has this kind of mentality. It is difficult for an individual to be able to leave up to their goals in events that they are scared. The other disadvantage of this form of mentality is that an individual would have a hard task of finding their passion in life.

Reasons Why Mindsets Matter

The common types of mindset across the globe are fixed and growth mindsets. It is because they comprise a greater percentage of the world population. These two forms of mindsets make people have a different way to react in their day-to-day life situations. Their difference in how these two groups of people perceive information that is presented to them.

We can narrow down the concept of how these groups respond to information differently. The fundamental difference can be measured by how they perform; this refers to their levels of productivity. People who are characterized by fixed mindsets tend to have an active reaction when presented with information about their performance levels. The level of performance can take different cases from education to work performance. This is a different case compared to people who are characterized by the development of the mindset. These people have a positive mental reaction when they are told that they can improve the results of their performance. Their approach to life events and results is often how they did it and what they can do to make the results of their performance to improve.

The mindset of an individual plays a critical role when they are handling the setbacks that life presents. There are several situations that life might present an individual that tends to be heartbreaking. People are characterized by handling these situations differently because of the varied types of mindsets that they possess. An individual with a fixed kind of mindset is likely to be highly discouraged in the event that they are faced with difficult life situations.

The major reason behind this problem of a fixed mindset person giving up is due to the fact that they may have trouble adapting to changing circumstances. Folks with fixed mindset, while open-minded (unless they are too set in their ways) will sill have trouble adapting to change simply because they are not wired that way. In contrast, folks with a growth mindset may take setbacks in stride on move on. Individuals with a fear mindset tend to take setbacks very seriously to the point where they may feel like even a slight setback is a devastating blow.

Neuroplasticity

There are several studies that have shown that an individual can change their mindset. This is the good news that can be embraced by an individual who desires to change their mindset. The occurrence has been brought to the limelight in a medical field known as neuroscience. The studies in this field have been able to show that the mind of an individual continuously develops and changes with time when they grow and develops to become an adult. Therefore, it is true that an old dog has the potential to learn new tricks.

The brain of an individual can be compared to highly flexible material. The concept of the brain's plasticity depicts that an individual's brain has the potential to be reshaped at any time. The mind can be transformed in the form of different neural pathways. Neuroscientists have gone a notch higher by calling this phenomena neuroplasticity.

There are several people who are prone to questioning themselves about how a mindset transformation process is possible. The process of forming new neural paths of the brain is done by development or thinking in a different way that is specific with certain principles. The normal thing an individual says or does in their daily life has a big impact on this course. It is because they have a way in which they become wired to an individual's brain. This forms their habits which develop into a part of their character over time. They have a huge impact as this becomes the route to an individual's brain.

As such, we will be taking a look at how a mindset can be modified.

Steps to Changing Mindsets

There are several things that can motivate an individual to change their mindset. The most common reason is to accomplish specific goals in their life. These steps for changing one's mindset include:

1. Thinking of Mindset as a Voice

There are several ways that a mindset can manifest itself in an individual. It is critical for an individual to realize how they recognize or talk to themselves in private. It is because this is the root of their mindset's manifestation. The truth is that you ought to pay keen attention to your own thoughts, and if there are any that are seen to hinder your potential, such thoughts ought to be removed from your mindset.

2. Choosing Growth

This step is easy when an individual has recognized the thoughts that hinder them from achieving success. This step involves an individual understanding and analyzing challenges, criticism, and setbacks. They are then tasked to choose the path that betters them. Doing so involves stretching the abilities of an individual.

3. Talking Back

This quality is very important at the moment an individual wants to clear the voices in their head. When situations seem to be tough, a person can choose to reframe the situation and look at the positive side. It is the belief that promotes the growth and development of an individual's mindset. In way, it is looking at setbacks and laughing in their face especially when circumstances seem daunting. While it it not intended to make fun of a serious situation, it is intended to give you the leverage you need over a conflictive matter.

4. Acting out your Plans

This step is one of the most difficult steps since you, as an individual, area meant to improve their thoughts. The process entails a person changing the script that was in their head both in thought and action. Some folks tend to be challenged by the thought of confronting their personal voice. Yet, you can flip the script and let your inner voice reveal what it truly wants to achieve. At the end of the day, you will be able to place the right script in your mind thereby allowing you to become what you truly want to be.

Chapter 2 Understanding Panic Attacks

What Is A Panic Attack?

A panic attack can be defined as an abrupt and quick onset of fear, which can be extremely unpleasant, uncomfortable, and frightening. It is also described as the point at which the body's inbuilt alarm system is activated. When there is a panic attack, the body's inbuilt alarm system is powered by adrenaline and helps to increase blood flow, heart rate and breathing. It also helps in responding and reacting to impending danger. This danger response system, in some individuals, work perfectly well, but in some others, it is blown out of proportion in relation to whatever the stress is. In simpler terms, panic attacks are a type of fear response and are just one of the common phenomenons everyone gets to experience at a point in their lives. As panic attacks are higher than normal response to excitement, danger or stress, they can be viewed as being traumatic. A typical panic attack peaks in approximately 10 minutes, and it is characterized by a host of symptoms. Panic attacks, which can be called anxiety, in response to specific causes, can come on quickly and alternatively for no just reason. Following the establishment that these panic attacks are spontaneous, certain people have these sudden attacks that span several minutes, while others may last longer. These attacks are common, and as such, can reoccur when there is an increase in the level of distress, which in turn affects our lives in ways that cause serious harm to the body. Although they are extremely unpleasant, uncomfortable and frightening experiences, they are responsive to a treatment, which serves as a light in a dark tunnel. You must understand that anxiety is a physiological reaction that takes place in the body. Anxiety is also a response to stress. However, stress is a threat to our body. Our ancestors felt anxious and nervous in the face of danger, and these body responses acted as security systems kept them in check. Realistically, if you are faced with real imminent danger, for example, you are faced with a wild beast, you need to have an instantaneous reaction that would keep you far from this danger. This means your body needs to step on it to keep you safe. This adrenaline is usually the fuel your body needs to escape these situations, but sometimes the body's security alarm is triggered by a false alarm, and our stress levels reach its peak point with no real threat and this triggers a panic attack.

What Triggers Panic Attack?

Triggers for panic attacks are dominantly stressful and terrifying situations. For example, certain stress factors at work can activate the emergency response system, because the body identifies it as threatening, even though in the real sense of it, direct risk to survival is absent. Sometimes, the natural 'fight or flight' emergency response system activates when there is no particular danger in sight, which is a pointer to the fact that some panic attacks are not triggered by anything. Questions posed are based around why the body enters an emergency mode in the absence of real danger. More often than not, most people are more terrified by the physical response their body produces as a result of the emergency response system. These physical sensations could include tightness in your chest and shortness of breath, which in turn alarms you and gets you thinking wild like 'Am I having a heart attack?' or ' Am I going to faint?' The mind is then driven to believe that there is danger when, in the real sense, there is no real danger. Sometimes, that leads to a full-blown panic attack. It is said that humans cause panic attacks by themselves because they misinterpret physical symptoms as signs of impending death, craziness, loss of control, embarrassment, or even fear. One important thing concerning panic attacks and anxiety is, they occur randomly in response to initial sensations without thoughts of danger making you alarmed and afraid. After having one or more panic attacks, you start to focus more on what goes on in your body, thus panic occurs automatically without your control. At this point, you become very focused on discovering different symptoms that tell the beginning of an attack. This, in turn, paves way for constant panic attacks to happen as you notice certain changes that ordinarily you would not have noticed and think them to be threatening. Continuous panic attacks are referred to as panic disorders, and sometimes they run in families while at other times, no one has any idea why they occur. The level of chemicals in the brain also plays a part in causing panic disorder. That is shown through the fact that some various medications and treatments that help to balance chemical levels, help to alleviate symptoms of panic attack. Science has evolved, and researchers have proposed and developed new therapies and treatments that help in correcting these disorders. Examples of how these therapies had to do with patients and individuals deciding to take part in certain clinical trials to find treatments for different people and different symptoms and they usually are free. Scientists learn more about how the brain works and what treatment works for certain symptoms.

Constant panic attacks make you live in fear of more attacks, which in turn makes you begin to avoid things you think would trigger these attacks. It breeds a negative effect as you begin to go through life looking for situations that would trigger these attacks, which leaves you always on guard. Think about you trying to skydive from an airplane, with so many details and all the right conditions and factors required. Ask yourself how you would feel before this adventure. To help you out here, I would list a couple of signs and sensations you would feel, and they include, faster heart racing and heart-pounding, your legs start to shake and quiver, your palms start to sweat, and you almost seem unable to catch your breath as your thoughts run wild. Other symptoms begin to also emerge, like your mouth feeling dry with the fear of you throwing up. You can literally see yourself from outside your own body, as you start to doubt the fact that you are actually about to jump off the plane. Then imagine once again when all these sensations were at their peak, and you are then automatically transported to a much calmer situation or a less dangerous scenario.

Panic Attack Types.

There are different categories of thoughts that cause panic attacks, and as such, they are grouped into the panic attack types. They include;

Type 1: Overestimating

This type occurs more often when we think something that ordinarily does not happen would happen, and we get scared. For example, the overall feeling we get that we would faint or die during a panic attack is overestimating. Overestimating is usually connected to physical fears like fainting, hurting oneself, having a heart attack or even dying. In this case, we tend to overthink and exaggerate certain feelings and this causes our body to go into overdrive. Illustration: What is it that would make me afraid in case I have panic attack? It possible I won't be able to breathe in adequate air. At this point, what would happen? Death might be eminent.

Type 2: Catastrophizing

Catastrophizing involves imagining the worst possible thing that would occur and cause panic attacks, and our inability to cope in scenarios like that. For example, if If I fall on these stairs, I would embarrass myself, and everyone would laugh at me or ill freak out and go crazy with no one helping me. In contrast to overestimating which is a result of the physical construct, catastrophizing is often related to the social construct. An example of catastrophizing is, 'What am I afraid will happen when I have a panic attack? I'll be terrified. What would be so bad about feeling scared? Sometimes, I do pass out in the processing of getting scared. What is not so good regarding that? It will draw peoples' attention to me and my situation. So, what tends to happen next? Even though some might be empathetic, some might still laugh at the situation.

To help yourself in overcoming overestimating and catastrophizing, questions one should ask themselves are, 'what would be so bad about this situation?', 'what would it lead to'? And what happens next after the scenario?

TACKLING CATASTROPHIZING?

To overcome these types of panic attacks, questions need to be asked. 'What is the worst that can happen, and what steps do I need to take to cope? 'How bad is it? 'Will it really affect my life in a year from now?' , 'Have I been embarrassed before?', 'How did it turn out? 'Did it make a difference? These are few questions that could help to allay worries. It is quite important we understand that these things we fear are hassles and not horror and we can always cope with the situations.

Symptoms Of Panic Attack

There are a number of different symptoms of panic attacks that you may suffer from. In fact, you may suffer from any combination of these symptoms or even all of them. It can be a very terrifying and emotional experience and it's something that you can't forget and likely live in fear of happening again. Understanding a little more about these symptoms may be able to help you when we get to how you can overcome them and the panic attacks in general.

Shortness of Breath

Shortness of breath may feel like (or actually be) hyperventilating. You'll feel like you just can't get a good breath and you just don't know what to do. The fear of not being able to breath is often cause for increased hyperventilation in many instances. The important thing is trying to catch your breath (understandably quite difficult during a panic attack). Being able to calm your breathing is actually going to help with a lot of the symptoms that we're going to talk about here, but it's going to take a lot of work to be able to do this during your panic attacks. No one is going to tell you this is going to be an easy process.

Heart Palpitations

Anotherproblem that arises when you suffer from a panic attack is heart palpitations. What this feels like is your heart is racing. It starts beating much faster than normal and, no matter what you do, you can't slow it down. This affects your breathing as well and by controlling your breathing you may be able to relax your heartbeat. Of course, these palpitations could be mild or they could be strong.

Chest Pain

Many people mistake their panic attacks for a heart attack because of all the symptoms that come along with both. A panic attack can even result in chest pain just like a heart attack and, in serious cases, it can actually result in heart problems. It's important to pay attention to your symptoms and to get help right away if you think there may be something serious going on. In many instances, with proper treatment, individuals can learn ways to determine whether they are having a real medical emergency or if they are having a panic attack. This way they know how to treat the problem.

Trembling/Shaking

Because of all the adrenaline that runs through your body during a panic attack (part of the fight or flight response) you may experience trembling and shaking while you're experiencing other symptoms. This symptom can be serious as well, causing violent trembling, or it may be relatively mild, shaking as though you were cold. The good news is, unless you fall or bump into something, this type of trembling is highly unlikely to cause any type of health problems. You are not likely to suffer adversely from this symptom.

Choking

Sometimes your panic attacks may feel as though your throat is closing up, resulting in even more trouble breathing. Because you are likely hyperventilating and still not getting enough air, it feels like you're choking, like there's not enough air out here for you. This can be a terrifying feeling and it's something to work with. Choking from lack of air can really happen during a panic attack and you may find yourself struggling to get the air you need simply to stay conscious. If you are eating or drinking something (sometimes it will be recommended that you get a drink of water or anything else) this can become even more dangerous.

Feeling Detached

It may feel as though you are not actually part of what's going on. You may feel completely detached either from the situation that is happening around you or from yourself entirely. These feelings of detachment are often the way that your body attempts to deal with the situation that it is in. By detaching you from the situation however, your body is making it more difficult for you to come to terms with what is going on. You feel as though you have no control over the situation and therefore that you are stuck with whatever is happening, which can be even more frightening.

Sweating

Sweating will often come along with trembling and with the hot and cold flashes we'll mention as well. You may start sweating for a variety of reasons. It may start because of the sudden changes in temperature (the flashes) or it may happen because you are nervous or frightened. Trying to keep your temperature regulated becomes very difficult when you are suffering from a panic attack but it is definitely going to be important. You won't suffer too adversely from sweating (unless it goes on excessively and you become dehydrated) but it can be difficult to work with.

Nausea

As your heart starts to race and your breathing becomes difficult you will likely also experience problems with nausea. Because your adrenaline is kicking up this is a common response that your body has. The adrenaline that courses through your system during a panic attack, if not used up, is not good for your body. This is actually what can cause you to feel sick and it can cause you to actually be sick as well. This is uncomfortable and difficult to deal with but it isn't necessarily dangerous (unless it goes on for a long time).

Dizziness/Lightheadedness

Now because you're feeling like you can't catch your breath it can be difficult to get enough air in. When you don't have enough air in your lungs and getting to your brain it can be difficult to remain functioning properly. You suffer from the lack of oxygen and this causes you to feel dizzy or lightheaded. The only way to overcome this is to sit down and take the time to breathe deeply. It's difficult to do this when you're suffering from a panic attack, but it's the only way the process is going to work.

Hot/Cold Flashes

Hot and cold flashes are quite common as well, especially because you have difficulty with breathing properly and may experience sweating as a result of the fear you face. Because of that sweating you will feel excessive hot flashes followed by excessive cold flashes as well. Trying to recover from this can be difficult and you'll definitely need to in order to resolve any potential health problems. Having these flashes for too long can result in problems for your health and you may end up feeling more nauseous.

Fear of Dying/Going Crazy

The biggest part about panic attacks is that most people believe that they are going crazy or that they are going to die. The feelings that go along with the panic attack itself are extremely intense and they tend to feel as though they are never going to survivethe experience. This is a terrifying feeling and you want to make sure that you're doing everything you can to improve it. This is the biggest reason that you have trouble with panic attacks and they are the part of the entire experience that is going to make you feel the worst about everything.

Chapter 3 Identifying Negative Thoughts

Nearly everybody has experienced two kinds of thoughts. These forms of thoughts are one that offers encouragement and also critics an individual. These forms of thoughts are always with people nearly in a day to day basis. They have the potential to affect the day an individual has since they shape our perception of things and experiences life offers. The focus is vehemently drawn to the negative form of thoughts that is also known as the gremlin. The effect this form of thinking has to an individual is detrimental. Especially when this form of thoughts keep on recurring day in day out.

There are several steps that an individual can use to identify this form of thoughts. The steps are divided into two parts.

1. Identification of the running commentary running in one's head

The best depiction can be used by a movie. There are certain movies which have audio commentary tracks that run in them. There are situations that an individual is immersed in watching what the director and the actors are saying, there are other moments when an individual focus only on what is happening on the screens. The inner thoughts in an individual brain at times behave the same way. There are several thoughts that crisscross the mind even if an individual does not pay attention. These thoughts have a very important influence on how an individual perceives several things. Therefore, it is very critical for an individual to pause and just have a take at the commentary in his or her brain.

2. Accept the thoughts if they are negative

The inner thoughts of a normal human being cannot be supportive and positive all the time. Various people who experience anxiety attacks are prone to experiencing this form of negative thoughts. There are certain that bed thoughts are justified however; an individual is discouraged from these episodes. The common moments that these form of thoughts can be justified. A good example is an individual who is about to cliff to cliff dive and motivates him or herself to do the activity despite not knowing to swim. However, these thoughts are discouraged when an individual is about to do an easy test and he or she thinks he or she won't pass.

3. Using individual feeling as the cue for examining one's thoughts

There are several moments that people cannot have themselves attuned to our thoughts. People can be listeners to their thoughts for a long time and get nothing done. However, there are several emotional signs that negative thoughts can seem to portray. These feelings are very important when portrayed and need examination. These moments are associated with an individual being anxious or worried. Once these emotions are portrayed, an individual can start the process of examining his or her thoughts.

Through paying close attention, he or she can eventually peruse a right course of action.

1. Figuring out if one is filtering

The negative form of thinking can be derived from several forms of topics in the current globe. It is predicted to be derived from a familiar set of general forms. One of these forms is described as filtering. The form of filtering comes into play when an individual secludes positive thoughts from negative thoughts in certain situations. After secluding these thoughts, an individual then picks to handle things with negative thoughts. An elucidation can be used by an individual who has won the lottery. The ideology of filtering comes in to play when this individual only thinks about taxes, fee to be paid to financial advisors and hand out to be given to friends.

2. Perceive if one is personalizing

There are several instances when a person can blame him or herself. An individual can blame himself, for example, blaming the rain because he or she wanted to go out. A person can also take it out on sports saying a certain team always loses when he or she watches. The two depictions are the best elucidation of what we talk about as personalizing things. It is a bad form of handling unwanted emotions when an individual blames him or herself. A person can also blame him or herself in an instance when his or her parents' divorce. The common form of thought is crossing an individual's mind is maybe he or she is the reason they were not happy.

3. Catching oneself catastrophizing

This moment entails a person anticipating the worst of thing to happen in life. Such thoughts include an individual predicting that it may rain during the wedding day; he can anticipate that he or she won't be able to park the vehicle accurately or he or she will die alone. It is not bad when an individual is preparing for the worst things to happen. But is a bad case when an individual is experiencing these thoughts amid of contrary evidence. This is a depiction of having negative thoughts.

4. Picking up the habit of polarizing

There are several people who have a different perception of themselves and the world surrounding them. The perception is normally in a rigid binary fashion. The binary fashion includes seeing things either good or bad, white or black and yes or no. People who exemplify this form of thoughts tend to complicate various things because they don't have middle grounds. People who have the thought of polarizing effect only seething as either failure or success.

5. Judging if one is umping into conclusions

This is a form of negative thinking and is similar to drawing assumptions to the negative side. The occurrence entails having the worst case of thoughts to an event even before their outcome is released. These situations do not provide any reason for an individual to having such thoughts. People tend to predict the worst case if they did a mistake during an interview. However, it is advisable for an individual to remain patient until the outcome is witnessed.

6. Observing if one is self-limiting

An individual can limit his or her chances of succeeding by creating a self fluffing prophecy. The process of self-fulfilling prophecy is created when an individual already makes up his or her mind before completion of anything. The thought of self-limiting comes in to play from negative thoughts that limit someone's potential artificially. This poses a bigger threat to a person's personal achievements and happiness.

7. Homing in one's habits of speech

There are several bad habits that are created by negative thinking by an individual. People might not realize what they say at the moment but it comes to be detrimental in the future. A good depiction occurs when an individual calls him or herself stupid after committing a mistake. If this action is done several times, it has to push someone's image internally with time. It is because it develops as a normal assumption with time.

8. Observing how one makes other people's thoughts his or her own

When an individual is always blamed about every mistake he or she does, or during corrections is told he or she owed to do certain things; it proves to be a worse case in the future. This is despite an individual holding on to the advice. It is because the words and thoughts from external environment affect a person. They make an individual have negative thoughts of guilt.

Chapter 4 Emotions And Anxiety

As already mentioned, there is a direct relationship between emotions and anxiety. The human brain draws a relationship from your previous experiences and associates them with your current life experiences. Painful emotional instances in the past may, in a big way, affect your life at every level. For this reason, emotions must be kept in check at all times.

What Emotions Are?

There are many definitions of the word emotion in psychological terms. According to psychologist Don Hockenbury, emotions refer to a complex psychological state that entails three components: subjective response, the psychological response, and expressive response. Although this definition may sound complex, it captures the details of the word emotions. An emotion is a process and not an instance. An emotion is triggered through both psychological processes after a subjective action to bring forward the expressive element. Psychologists believe that emotions refer to mental reactions to a subjective matter. Painful instances often cause negative emotions. Any action that may impact pain on your brain will lead to negative emotions, which may be expressed through various expressive means.

To understand emotions, let's look at the three subjective components of emotions and how they affect our lives.

The Physiological Response

You have probably felt your heart skip a bit or your stomach lurch when you are in fear. An experience that may instill fear, such as someone startling you from behind, always causes a psychological response. Most psychologists believe that emotions and psychological reactions are felt simultaneously. On the other hand, some believe that the psychological reaction is the process of emotion. In either case, a strong psychological reaction is part of the emotion. A Person may experience different psychological reactions during emotions such as sweating palms, increased heartbeat, trembling, among others. These reactions may be very intense in some people, while in others, they are barely noticeable.

No one can control the psychological impact of emotions. When someone is emotional, he may be seen sweating or trembling uncontrollably. It may take a few minutes for the person to regain a normal psychological state. The autonomic nervous system in the human body controls emotions. It controls the natural flow of blood in the body, the digestive system, and all the activities of your body that depend on blood flow. It also caters to the fight or flight reaction. The fight or flight reaction instinctively causes some to fight or run away when there is a threat.

The subject of emotion is one that still needs a lot of research. Psychological reactions to emotions have been linked with the automatic response system. However, recent studies now show that the brain has an important role to play in emotional, psychological reactions. Brain scans show that the limbic system of the brain plays a significant role in emotions, especially fear. It is important to note that every action on the brain may cause and impact, which may also result in an emotional reaction.

The Subjective Experience

While it is a fact that the expression of emotions is universal, research also shows that emotions are affected by our life experiences. The experiences of a person from childhood may affect the reactions negatively.

For example, everybody reacts negatively when angry. However, the dimensions of the reaction vary from one person to another, depending on the cultural factors or subjective experiences of a person as an individual. The expression of anger in one person may be a mild annoyance while another person may react with violence.

Another factor to consider is that emotions are not absolute. You cannot tell which factors cause which types of emotions completely. For instance, if you are starting a new job, you may experience emotions of fear, nervousness, and excitement at the same time.

Different circumstances may trigger different emotions. Some emotions may last for as long as a day or even a week, while others may last just a few seconds. For instance, if someone tells you something funny, it may trigger happiness just for a moment. On the other hand, if someone tells you a compliment on your job or career, you may stay happy for the whole day. In other cases, if you are expecting a child, you may experience mixed emotions such as excitement and nervousness. These emotions may last for as long as two weeks.

The Behavioral Response

The other component of emotions is the behavioral aspect. This is the most visible aspect of emotions. The expressive component mainly refers to the physical and expressive actions taken by a person when they feel a certain emotion. The expressions for emotions are universal, although the intensity varies from one person to another. We can read and understand people's emotions by observing their actions and expressions. In psychology, the ability to observe and interpret other people's emotions is tied to the subject of emotional intelligence. As we will see later, emotional intelligence plays an integral part in retraining your brain.

The interpretation of body language and facial expressions helps us understand people's emotions. Social-cultural norms also have a place in determining people's expressions. Emotions may be displayed or may be muffled within. Emotionally intelligent people tend to have control over emotion and may work hard not to show the expressions associated with certain emotions. For example, in Japan, people are expected to mask their feelings of fear or disgust in the presence of a senior person. A person who grew up under such a culture may never show true emotions of fear and disgust. These social-cultural differences may sometimes make it difficult to interpret people's emotions across cultures.

Some individuals show a strong intensity when expressing emotions. Some racial groups have been associated with aggressive intensity when responding to negative emotions. Emotions may be intense in some people, leading to tears, weakness in the body to the extent of passing out. In other individuals, the emotions are only mild and may just be visible through facial expressions.

What Causes Emotions

Emotions are such a complex subject that there seems to be little agreement among psychologists on how they are formed. Many theories try to explain the concept of emotions and how they are formed. One of the outstanding theories on the formation of emotions was first published by an American psychologist in 1842. According to psychologist William James, emotions are formed through a two-step process, which includes physical changes in the body and interpretation of the changes by a person.

To understand how emotions are formed, we must have an understanding of human physiology. It is suggested that emotions are the extra ingredient that makes humans special. However, this may not be very true, considering that all other animals also experience emotions. The only difference between humans and animals is that humans have many ways of expressing their emotions.

The emotional process starts with a chemical process within the body. Adrenaline, sometimes referred to as epinephrine, is a hormone released in response to panic, anger, and fear. It is the key hormone that activates the flight and fight mode in human beings. In other words, when something threatening occurs to someone, the hormone is released, prompting that person to react in defense or flight. Most emotions start with the release of hormones.

When a person perceives a threat within the mind, whether it is a real threat or an illusion, the body will be prompted to generate adrenaline. The generation of adrenaline leads to a series of chemical and physical changes. First, it leads to increased blood flow to the legs and the arms. It causes an increased heart rate and arouses all the senses to an alert state.

These occurrences may result in someone running away, showing aggression, or displaying fear. However, adrenaline only sparks negative emotions. On the other hand, happiness, joy, and excitement, among other positive emotions are formed depending on the release of several happiness hormones. Such hormones include dopamine- a hormone that is responsible for feelings of happiness, bliss, etc.

Cortex, the part of the brain responsible for sending out emotional signals, sends signals to the body prompting the release of dopamine. This, in turn, contributes to the feelings of bliss, euphoria, and pleasure. Happiness and joy are all aspects of pleasure and bliss.

The theory proposed by James Williams shared many principles with another theory proposed by Carl Lange, a Danish psychologist. Although their books were written independently, the two psychologists seemed to agree on the fact that a person only perceives that they are experiencing an emotion after the chemical and physical changes in the body.

It is still a big question to be answered why the body responds by producing chemicals. The reaction of the body is believed to start from the brain. In early studies of psychology, it was believed that emotions did not have a connection to the brain. However, more recent studies show a direct relationship between the brain and emotions. The brain responds in certain ways before the body makes chemical changes, which are then expressed outward as emotions.

A good example would be when someone is been involved in a road accident. First, the body experiences change due to a rush of adrenaline. The person then perceives the emotion' fear' after the outward expressions such as trembling and shaking. Most people cannot perceive their emotions before that outward expression. Expression of emotions includes many aspects that may vary in intensity depending on the person.

Relationship Between Emotions and Anxiety

The relationship between anxiety and panic attacks has been linked to:

Emotional scars: Emotional scars are wounds that have been deeply entrenched in your mind and your heart. Emotional scars are painful memories that are associated with certain people or events. These scars are the biggest cause of anxiety. If a person has been through emotional pain, the scars may take a long time to heal. For as long as the scars are still in place, it becomes difficult for that person to live life to the fullest. These scars are from time to time, a reminder that danger is around. For instance, if a person has been through an abusive relationship, he/she is constantly reminded that relationships can be abusive. Even if you are not in an abusive relationship, you may find yourself associating every relationship with abuse. Such emotional memories may lead to fear and worry. When you have an emotional scar, you constantly fear that the people who caused it may reappear again and cause you the same harm.

Emotional Triggers: Emotional triggers are factors that relate to your past emotional experiences. If you have suffered abuse before, you may be triggered to remember the experiences that cause emotional pain by some triggers. The triggers will cause you to remember all the painful moments you went through. Most people who experience panic attacks are affected by emotional triggers. For instance, if you have undergone sexual abuse, you may experience panic attacks after watching a movie that entails rape. If you see something that directly relates to your negative emotional experiences, you may find yourself suffering from negativity.

Current Emotional Experiences: Your current emotional experiences may also lead to anxiety and panic attacks. In cases where you experience the loss of a loved one through a tragic event, you may experience panic attacks due to the devastating state of emotions. In fact, most people only experience panic attacks and anxiety when they are under such emotional conditions. The emotional environment cultivates a good ground for anxiety and panic attacks to crop in. During sorrowful moments, loss, and pain, you must strive to remain within your mind. Friends and family also must console people who are around them. If you do not take control of your emotions, they may slowly escalate, leading to anxiety and panic attacks.

How To Control Your Emotions

Emotional control is an important skill that will not only help you deal with your social life but will help you manage conditions such as anxiety and panic attacks. One important factor to note is that emotional control is not the same as emotional suppression. In fact, you must never suppress your emotions. In all circumstances, you must ensure that you find a healthy way of expressing your emotions. Negative emotions can be expressed positively. If you want to completely gain control over your feelings, think about emotions as a form of energy.

Emotions are just a form of energy that tries to find a way out of the body. When the energy is negative, you may see expressive actions such as aggression, shouting, etc. Such emotions may influence your actions and daily activities, making it difficult for you to live your life happily. However, if you master the art of emotional control, you do not have to worry about the negative energy. Through emotional control, you can stop all the negative emotions before they happen.

The best way to control emotions is to find an alternative way of emotional expression. Painful emotions such as anger and bitterness can still be expressed through civilized ways. Some of the civilized ways of emotional release include singing, dancing, exercise, among others. Some individuals opt to exercise or punch a punching bag instead of getting violent. As a civilized person, you must lookout for the best ways possible to express your emotions. When you release your emotions, you also get rid of emotional scars that might cause you pain in the future. Letting your emotions out will help you stay in your mind and have strong control over every situation of life, which is the only way out in dealing with panic disorders and anxiety. Some of the ways of controlling your negative emotions include:

Use a journal to track your emotions: Emotions occur in our lives daily. However, if you are not even aware of the emotions occurring in your life, you may not be in a position to control them. A journal may help you track your emotions. Later on, we will look at emotional awareness and how to sharpen your awareness skills.

Name your feelings: Naming your feelings requires that you add a tag to every moment in life. Every experience you go through gives you a certain feeling. Naming your feelings is still a part of emotional awareness that will help you overcome your negative feelings. When you name your feelings, you can detect the negative ones. If someone says something to you, you should be aware enough to label the comment as either negative or positive. This is the only way to get to the root of your fears and anxiety.

Do not suppress your emotions: The main reason why people plunge into anxiety and panic attacks is that they work so hard to stop their emotions. There is nothing wrong with controlling with your feelings; however, suppressing them entirely is not advisable. If you suppress your emotions, you will eventually lead to a pileup of negative energy in your body. The negative energy explodes once in a while through panic attacks. Although you may not understand it, the main reason why panic attacks occur is that there are plenty of emotions bottled up on the inside.

Focus on your dreams: If you are trying so hard to control your emotions, but you keep on failing, note down your dreams, and choose to focus on them. We only pay too much attention to feel when our minds are not preoccupied. If you are always free with nothing essential to pursue, you will focus on every negative word said to you. You will take a lot of time thinking about the negative terms of people and even start cultivating them in your mind. This may lead to the growth of negativity. If you wish to be successful as an individual, you must get rid of all negative emotions by focusing on your dreams and future. Working towards your future sets your mind free and allows you to concentrate.

Listen to your emotions: The other way to control your emotions is simply paying attention to what your body wants. Most times, we are quick to blame others when we experience emotional pain and disappointment. When we are in emotional distress, we seek revenge or to pass the pain to another person. In reality, feeling sad or fear is not bad. All emotions allow us to scrutinize our feelings, thoughts, and desires. If you are in a place where you are experiencing fear, you should take the opportunity and examine yourself. Try finding out what your body wants and why your body is driving you into feelings of sadness. Every emotion gives us an opportunity to learn. You can learn new facts about your strengths and abilities.

Practice Vulnerability: Most people only stay in their emotional pain because of the fear of sharing it. If you share your emotional situation, you become vulnerable. You have to express your weaknesses and let the world know your fears. Although you may think that expressing your weaknesses is a bad thing, you have it all wrong. In today's world, everybody craves authenticity. Most people are living behind masks. It is only a few who come out and publicly speaks about their fears that are embraced. The world is looking for individuals who are strong enough and willing to stand up to their fears. If you are suffering under negative emotions, you must stand up and become strong by sharing your fears and emotional distress.

Healthy Coping Mechanisms: Lastly, you can control your emotions and stay in control by employing some healthy coping mechanisms. We have already mentioned that there are alternative ways of emotional expression. If you do not want to be under emotional sabotage and be controlled by your own emotions, you have to find alternative emotional control options. You have to look at other ways of controlling your emotions.

Alternative Ways Of Emotional Expression

Musical Expression: Musical expression is a way of letting your emotions out through music. Different types of music can affect our emotions. For instance, when you are stressed, you can relax the pressure on your mind by listening to mind soothing music. Such music will help you calm your nerves and start thinking soberly. The soothing music includes gentle instrumental songs such as Jazz, R$B, and blues, among others. Such songs target the three brainwaves (Theta, Beta, and Gama). When you listen to different types of music, you can either calm the mind or stimulate the mind. For instance, high tempo music or feel-good music may make you feel light and free. It is common for people to go out for parties after a stressful day at work. Music helps reverse most of the effects caused by stressful workmates.

Controlled Breathing: You can also bundle up your emotions in your breathe and push them out. When people are angry, it is common to see a person taking in a deep breath. This deep breath can be used to harness all the negative energy in the body and push it out. Through a simple meditation technique, just breathe in and hold your breath. With your mind focused on all the areas of pain, collect the physical and emotional pain, and push it out. If you choose to collect the pain and push it out through your breath, you reduce the chances of having the scars stay in your body forever.

Practice Physical Exercises: The other way of getting rid of emotions is exercising. Exercises will help you clean your body of any negative thoughts. When you focus on cardiovascular exercises, you balance the flow of blood in the body and keep your mind distracted from negative thoughts. Most people who have suffered from panic attacks before tend to avoid exercising. This is not the right approach. Even if you have undergone painful instances in your life, you cannot conclude that exercise will lead to the same. In fact, cardiovascular exercises lower the chances of panic attacks. Do not be afraid of getting into the gym, thinking that panic attacks may reoccur again. Get out there and engage in activities that will distract your thoughts.

Chapter 5 Routines And Positive Programming

Remember when we said that a big part of phobias was all about accustoming yourself to the idea that a specific thing is bad and then using various methods to back up this idea?

Has it occurred to you that you can literally do the exact opposite if you were so inclined?

Think about it—if you can figure out a way to teach your brain to have positive reactions to the same things you are afraid of or, if not have positive reactions, at least be neutral toward them, you eliminate the cause of anxiety all together!

Hello, positive programming!

Another thing that actually helps quite a bit is developing a thorough routine. With routines, you develop a sense of security and tend to inherently form habits, both things that help calm your panicked mind.

C. Recovery from Trauma

or a Traumatic Experience

Welcome to the official trauma vortex. Interesting way to refer to trauma, isn't it? The term "trauma vortex" was actually coined by bestselling author Jenni Schaefer. She came up with it when she was attempting to put into words what it was like for her to actually recover from post-traumatic stress disorder (PTSD). When describing her experience with PTSD, she once said, "PTSD told me this over and over again: 'You're not safe. You never will be. Being dead would be better than living one more day like this.' The message from my illness was clear: 'Give up.'"

Sadly, this doesn't just describe trauma and its aftereffects for her. In so many ways, this is what trauma has done to all its victims. In fact, PTSD is common in at least a fifth of all adults who have experienced trauma, making it one of the most common forms of trauma in existence.

How does one recover from it? Trauma-based recovery is significantly different from other panic disorders, particularly when it comes to the recovery process. Broadly speaking, though, the recovery falls under five major categories.

Impact and Stabilization

The initial impact of the trauma plays a big role in the subsequent panic it induces. What some people tend to forget is that the impact doesn't have to be direct for trauma to occur. In fact, passive impact, where an individual has witnessed a trauma as opposed to having experienced it, is just as common as direct trauma and can display identical symptoms. The trick to dealing with this issue of impact is by ensuring that you focus on stabilization.

Identify the range of emotions the trauma has left you feeling. These start from shock over the occurrence of the incident combined with fear of it happening again to helplessness that you were powerless to do anything to stop or prevent the incident and even guilt over your failings. Impact emotions are often followed by anxiety and a sense of hypervigilance, and it is here that you need to step in and start normalizing the matter.

The only way to truly invoke proper stability would be to tackle these head-on. Identify the behavior patterns you see in yourself and then follow that up with habit reinforcement techniques that help you change them.

Re-establishment of a Sense of Safety

The impact of the incident then results in the rescue of the victim. The problem is there is a time gap between the occurrence of the incident and the rescue, and within this time, we find that the individual is bombarded with a multitude of feelings—fear and anxiety being the most obvious ones.

Uncertainty, confusion, despair, denial, and then hopelessness— all these feelings begin to take root and, in doing so, shake the individual's sense of safety. This is where you try implementing the safety cards we've talked about earlier. Remember proper use of safety cards can help promote a strong self of well-being and help override the residual damages incurred from impact and rescue.

Mourning

Next up is mourning, where individuals deal with trauma and loss. A natural part of the healing process has to be mourning—

time for the individual to reflect and accept that they have, indeed, suffered a loss. Acknowledgment of this loss and then subsequent grief may seem like a painful burden to most survivors, but in truth, it is a critical part of the healing process.

As the individual accepts and grieves their loss, their brain begins to acknowledge and try to move forward. In contrast, by ignoring or burying the issue, what you are actually doing is letting the wound fester. Don't. Be human. Be brave and face your issues. Don't run away from them.

Recovery

And finally, we hit upon the issue of recovery. Since trauma-based recovery is such a sensitive topic, it is important to note that the recovery is twofold.

On the one hand, we deal with the initial recovery of basic faculties, ensuring that the individual in question is competently capable of taking care of their basic needs, such as their ability to take care of their own health and safety, taking care of food needs, maintaining a job and minimum social interaction.

However, following this, we need to zone in a little more on issues like fear, resentment, and depression—all issues that tend to have deep roots in victims of trauma. Start by identifying the core issues. What is the problem? What led to the problem? What is making you feel this anger? Once you've identified them, move on to asking if you can take any responsibility for the issues you've earmarked. What was your stake, and what did you do or fail to do?

Once you've been able to do that, you can actually open up to yourself and admit why this issue has scared you—what your loss has been. And finally, move on. You can either hold on to something that you can't change and spend years wailing and bemoaning the unfairness of the situation or chalk it down to life and move forward. There are always better thing waiting for you, and even if they aren't better, they are still there, so reach out!

D. Recovery from Worry and Guilt

Another major panic attack protagonist is the concept of worrying or unnecessary and pointless self-inflicted distress. Worry is a major trigger point for anxiety while stressors tend to play major roles in the introduction of causes. Worry is like salt to the wound and has a tendency to both agitate and instigate panic.

But worry isn't the only villain in this tale. Meet guilt, worry's equally dramatic and annoying cousin. If worry seems to use altruism to explain why they are causing such a ruckus, guilt uses manipulation to showcase its goods. Guilt and shame go hand in hand. Guilt clears the path for self-blame, giving you a clean shot, and then for good measure, drags you in shame to reinforce the negative bias it has carefully cultivated.

Obviously, this cannot be allowed to stand. Why don't we give you a few pointers on how to avoid these things?

Self-Empathy

First up, you have self-empathy—the ability to understand where your worry and guilt are stemming from—and being able to address it is a critical part of the recovery process. With self-empathy, you can open yourself up to deal with harsh truths and the root causes of your incessant worry and guilt. It is important to note though that self-empathy is not absolving in nature. You are meant to identify and try to understand your behavior patterns, not try to justify them!

Seeking Absolution

For absolution, we move on to the concept of forgiveness. People aren't perfect; they make mistakes, and sometimes these mistakes tend to take the form of harms inflicted on other people, either by direct or implied means. The problem with this is there are no take-backs in life. Once you've harmed someone, that harm is constant. It is a truth that you have to accept and live with, but what if you can't live with it? What if that guilt is eating you up from the inside and you have no one and nowhere to turn to.

Well then, you're being very selfish. In refusing to forgive yourself and, more importantly, in refusing to seek forgiveness, you are trying to retain control and decide what you deserve. What makes you think you get to do that? If you've made a mistake, you are on trial. You are not the judge. Your job is to acknowledge and repent and to do so in a way that means something. You don't get to just say, "Hey, I'm sorry." You need to explain exactly what you are sorry about. What did you do or fail to do? Why did you do it? When did you realize the impact of your actions? How did you attempt to fix it? All these questions are crucial to ensure you have chalked out a valid apology. Remember, holding in your feeling and brooding does nothing. It doesn't make you cool or a tortured hero. It makes you selfish.

Choose to be better. The people you've wronged deserve it.

E. Recovery from Criticism

Next up is criticism.

Nowadays, everyone's a critic, and guess who's sitting snugly at the top of the list?

Yup, you.

Not only are people their own worst critics, but they are also merciless when it comes to judging themselves. Every little thing you do is scrutinized and demeaned and devalued, but that's just you. With proper positivity training, you can and will overcome your tendency to inflict self-harm. What happens, though, when you are dealing with criticism from outside sources?

Not quite sure what I mean?

Think about your toxic work environment or those nagging family members who always seem to be waiting for you to put one step in the wrong. How do you deal with them? Because let's be honest, even though you want to shrug that stuff off, it's not as easy as it used to be. In fact, recently, it's been cutting deep, deeper than you care to admit, to the point where you are torn between running scared and fighting back, which is probably why you're just silently taking it.

Not a great feeling, is it?

Why don't we help you understand and defeat the bugger?

Reduce Validation Dependency

If you want to reduce your reactivity to criticism, you are going to have to start by reducing your need for validation. Let's rewind a bit. You listen to these things that your workmate or friend or family is telling you, don't you? You listen even though, for the most part, these comments and "critiques" have made you sad and resentful. In some cases, they've perhaps even induced self-violence. Have you ever wondered why you keep listening?

See It for What It Is

It's because deep down, you want someone to tell you that they're wrong. No matter who you are, no matter your stature or your achievements, confirmation that what you are doing is right and that who you are is commendable is an inherent need we all battle. It's like having an ego. No one really wants to admit to it, but it's there nonetheless. Being aware of this need that you have and finding a way to transform it into a want as opposed to a need is important. Stop judging yourself based on other people's standards. Be aware of yourself. Be aware of your actions, and judge them for yourself. You are all the validation you need.

Prune Your People

A great way to kick-start this new no-validation needed version of yourself is to take a hard look at the people you are surrounding yourself with and making a few quick adjustments.

Why?

Because at its core, criticism really isn't about you; it's about another person projecting their fears and failures on you. Your reactions, on the other hand, are all on you. Those are telling in that they show you how you feel and how aware you are of the consequences of your actions. By re-evaluating who you are surrounding yourself with, you are able to decide whether or not you are going to invite other people and their insecurities to take potshots at you. Yes, the fact that they are doing it from a flawed place means they need help, but you aren't ready to give them that help yet. All you are doing by staying here is hurting yourself. Stop, move away. Maybe someday things will be different, but for now, your focus needs to be you.

F. Recovery from Failure

In our race against time, to be successful and to have it all, we all tend to avoid talking about the elephant in the room. What happens when all that doesn't work out? Be logical. It's not really possible for someone to succeed at anything continuously all the time. You will or have, at some point, experienced failure. That's not even a question; it's a fact.

The only real question is, what do you do with failure? Also, how do you get past it?

Accept

For starters, as with any other stressor, you accept the situation. This can be particularly difficult when you are dealing with failure as there is a personal stake, and to admit and accept that you have failed also means that you are admitting and accepting that you and your efforts were not enough. And then once you start realizing that something you did failed, everything else in the world seems to snowball. All of a sudden, you are focused on how if your idea failed. You failed, and if you failed, you are a failure, and if you're a failure, you'll never amount to anything. It somehow doesn't seem to end.

Stop.

Breathe.

You need to start off by separating your failure from your sense of self. Your project or idea failed, but that does not mean you as a person has failed. As a person, your validation does not depend on any one thing, and if you continue to connect the two, what you're going to do is make it difficult for you to actually admit when you are wrong or when you are dealing with a sinking ship.

Being able to accept your failure at face value shows strength and courage, not insufficiency. Let's start here.

Apologize

Now move on to taking responsibility for your failures. Failures aren't on you, but taking responsibility for them and addressing them is!

You will often find that when dealing with failures, part of your guilt and panic comes from the fact that your failure may affect other lives. For instance, if you own a company and you made a bad decision that made it go bankrupt, your mistake has led to losses on the part of shareholders, investor, and even employees if it's bad enough.

That's a pretty heavy burden, but given that it is yours to bear, do it fast and do it well. Acknowledge the problem. Address it. Talk about how and where the problem occurred and why. But before you do any of that, apologize. Talk about your mistake, why it happened, and communicate your regrets. This is just as much for you as it is for others.

Address

Now that you're all done with the apologizing, move on and figure out a way to deal with the resulting problem. Remember, the issue isn't the problem; it's what you are going to do about the problem. Proactiveness is your new best friend!

Hasta La Vista

And finally, once you're done accepting, apologizing, and dealing with your problem, it is time for you to take the most important step of all—the one that takes you away from the issue. Once you have dealt with all that needs to be dealt with, you need to learn how to move away and move on from the problem. There is no need and no point in rehashing the same thing a million times. Let go and make room for new mistakes and successes.

G. Recovery from Shyness

Another pretty common anxiety disorder that easily morphs into panic is social anxiety, a.k.a. being shy. How bad is shyness? Pretty bad, to be honest. You see, shyness brings in a host of problems, including fear of crowds, fear of interacting with others. It's like phobia central—that's the bad news.

So, what's the good news?

Social anxiety also happens to be one of the easiest anxiety disorders to get over. It means once you have identified the source of the problem, which you have already done (obviously, because you're nodding as you read this—caught you in the act didn't we?), you can actually move on to solving the issue.

Off we go!

Pretend

So, the first thing you need to be prepared to do is act! Act your heart out. You are the new Rami Malek, and the stage is yours— the stage being life and the performance being your behavior, of course.

Confused?

When you pretend to be confident and extroverted, you can actually trick your mind into believing that you are, and in turn, you can actually become that person. It's like slipping into the skin of another person and staying there until some of the traits infuse into your own behavior pattern.

Pretty cool, isn't it? So, all you have to do now is pick someone you admire and aspire to be and emulate their behavior patterns. Oh, and while you're at it, you might want to say goodbye to the old you, just saying!

Practice

Okay, but pretending to be something isn't really enough, is it? You need to find a way to adopt these behavior patterns into yourself. After all, you want to adopt these particular behaviors. You don't want to be pretending to be this other person forever, right?

Well, frankly speaking, no. Of course, you don't want to be this other person. You want to be a better version of you! So, figure out what you need to do to be better and start working on it. For most people dealing with shyness, one of the major lackings that they identify within themselves is that because they tend to suffer from inferiority complexes, they have a hard time reaching out and mingling with other people. Well, work on it. Practice reaching out to two new people within a certain time. Make it a routine, something that you do every day or every week, and at the end of three months, you'll find that you are capable of doing it without breaking a sweat. Achievement unlocked!

Engage

The biggest mistake that people with social anxiety make is they tend to avoid people. The whole problem starts here and, unfortunately, gets reinforced here as well. You see, the more you avoid people, the more you are telling your mind that people are scary and need to be avoided, and then when you actually do it, you are reaffirming yourself that it's like your brain going, "See, I told you so!"

Now, first off, "I told you sos" are stupid. Don't let your brain get into that, but more importantly, how are you ever going to get over your fear of interacting with people if you aren't around people or, worse, if you are around them and deliberately avoiding them?

Be Vulnerable

This is where vulnerability kicks in.

Why aren't you willing to engage?

Because you're scared.

Why are you scared?

Because you are vulnerable. In putting yourself out there, you are opening yourself up to a vast array of issues, starting from betrayal to humiliation and all the other horrible things you can think of. I'll bet you have the latest Carrie reboot running through your head.

But aren't you forgetting something?

Isn't there a possibility that things will go well?

You see, when you open yourself up and let down your defenses, you are allowing people to see and interact with a side of you that they don't often get to see. Sure that means you could be made fun of and ridiculed, but you could also make lasting friends, and isn't that worth the risk?

Look, not everyone is going to love you. This doesn't speak to your character or who you are as a person at all, though—it's just life. People have different choices. They have different opinions, and they have different things that they like or dislike. They are not obliged to like you, and you are not obliged to care.

Be Persistent

You are, however, obliged to make a concentrated effort.

Why?

Because you owe it to yourself.

Look, things are tough, and you are going to want to quit and take the easy way out, or maybe you just want to crawl into a corner and cry your eyes out. Whatever the reason may be, giving up is the coward's way out.

That doesn't mean you can't take a break, though. If you ever feel like it's all too overwhelming for you, do that. Take a break, and take as many breaks as you need. Pace yourself. Slip, fall, and get back up.

But do get back up.

Your getting back up is what will determine whether or not you are going to be able to move past this disorder, and honestly, I for one believe you can. Someone who has the courage to identify that they have a problem and making an active choice to try to fix their problem is someone who is capable of moving mountains, and this, this isn't even a molehill.

Talk, Talk, Talk!

And that brings us to our final step—talking!

Why talking? Because effective communication is the key to all things. You see, the more you talk, the less you bottle up, so the lower your stress levels are. Pretty smooth, eh? But that's not all. At the same time, you are also ensuring that you are more engaged with the people around you and, as such, have a higher chance of being liked and understood.

Cool?

We're still not done!

Talking isn't a one-way street. When you talk to someone, you also listen to them in return, which means you are also building bridges that you can choose to cross whenever you feel comfortable. It is the perfect setup!

So, what are you waiting for? Get talking!

H. Recovery from Negative Self-Talk

Another prominent issue that you will find yourself dealing with is negativity and, in particular, negative self-talk. We've talked a little about this before in hen we were talking about how to deal with negativity.

The important thing you need to remember here is that even if you can silence the voices around you by selecting your companions, it's a little harder to silence the voice in your head. As you attempt to find your way out, remember to be kind and positive to yourself. Compassion and empathy will take you a long way, and you know what they say—charity starts at home!

I. The Importance of Mindfulness

And last but not least, mindfulness. Mindfulness is a magical tool. You see, in the rush of modern-day life and the madness it entails, so many of us have been sucked into this world where all we are doing is jumping from one task to another, and frankly, it's super exhausting!

And it's really hard to keep up with as well. This is why millennial burn out in such a big deal nowadays. Because everything we do is like a million things at once, yet it's still never enough.

Look, it's a jungle out there. Literally.

And while survival of the fittest is a grand concept, sometimes we probably need to take a step back and really evaluate what we have going on. What are our plans with our life? What do we want to achieve? Is it worth the sacrifices we are making?

Mindfulness deals with all this and more, because at its core, mindfulness teaches us to find focus both within ourselves and in our lives. So, what are you choosing today?

Chapter 6 The 6-Step Solution For Solving The Real Problem

I am now going to share with you my 6-step method for solving your panic attack problem, once and for all.

The first three steps are designed to improve your knowledge and understanding. Then, the final three steps are all action oriented.

The solution I'm going to suggest to you may seem counterintuitive at first glance, but it works nonetheless. At least it works for a great percentage of people who embrace it and have the courage to give it a try.

The reason it's counterintuitive is because your natural instincts for dealing with panic attacks haven't worked so far. In fact, they may have served to make your problem even worse.

In order to finally break free of your panic attacks, you are going to have to approach your problem differently. You are going to have to learn how to think differently and behave very differently.

Don't be worried, this is not hard to do, and I'm going to guide you in the process.

The solution I'm going to share with you is not new, nor did I invent it. It's been around for many years and thousands of people have applied it successfully. In fact, some people have used it to completely cure themselves of panic attacks, and a few of them suffered repeatedly from panic attacks for more than 30 years!

What is different, however, is the way I introduce you to this solution and the background of knowledge I'm going to give you (especially about the causes of your anxiety) that will help you both understand this solution deeply and embrace it with confidence.

So don't let the simplicity of this solution fool you—it's very powerful. You just have to understand why it's such a good approach (this is the purpose of the first three steps in the method), and then put it into action with the last three steps to get results.

So here we go. Be sure to read every word of these 6 steps before trying to apply this method. Don't skim or rush through this material or be super impatient to get your symptoms quickly reduced. Make sure you fully understand each step before moving on. And if you have trouble accepting any parts of this advice, have faith and keep reading on and absorbing the parts that do make sense to you. By the end of the full discussion, it may all come together for you.

Steps 1-3: Improving Your Understanding

Step 1. Understand The Nature And Causes Of Anxiety In All Human Beings

The first step in dealing with any anxiety problem is to understand the basic nature of anxiety and why it occurs for all human beings.

Fear (Anxiety) is a universal human emotion. Everyone has fears from time to time. Everyone has thoughts or life situations that cause them to feel afraid. And while the experience of fear can be different for each of us, common physical symptoms include:

Difficulty concentrating

Racing thoughts

Dizziness or lightheadedness

Dry mouth

Tightness in chest

Heart pounding or racing

Trouble breathing

Feeling hot or cold all over

Butterflies or pains in stomach

Nausea or diarrhea

Sweaty palms or armpits

Trembling hands or legs

Tingling feeling in arms or legs

Muscle tension

Feeling unsteady

Feeling like you're going to pass out

While most people who suffer from anxiety are very familiar with these and other anxiety-related symptoms, we are not always clear about what actually causes these feelings and body reactions to occur.

Mainly, we underestimate the role that our own internal fear-generating thoughts play in causing this common human emotion. As a consequence, we don't focus specifically on what these fear-generating thoughts have to be. Even worse, many of us have been taught to believe (by our society) that the external events which happen to us in life are the primary culprits causing us to feel afraid.

For example, you can falsely conclude, when you're having a panic attack, that it's your heart racing so fast that is making you feel so terrified. Or if you seem to start breathing very rapidly, you may think that it's this particular symptom that is causing your fears to escalate. Now, obviously, both of these physical sensations can be very scary, but it is not the physical sensations alone that are driving your panic.

You see, the real truth about fear (and most other human emotions) is that our emotions are never directly caused by anything that happens, either to us or around us. Fear is always the direct result of very specific internal thought patterns that also must be present (within us) before we can experience this emotion.

While it is certainly true that many things which happen to us or around us can trigger us to feel afraid, they cannot do this alone. They do it by triggering very specific internal thought patterns within us, which in turn give rise to our fears (and all their many physical manifestations), which we feel and perceive so acutely.

Thus, whenever you are feeling afraid or in a panic, there is a specific thought sequence or "thought program" that must have become activated within you. This same fear-producing thought sequence, in a very generic sense, is exactly the same for all human beings, regardless of nationality, language, or culture of origin.

KEY PRINCIPLE: Whenever a human being—any human being, including you—is feeling afraid, you have to be thinking in very predicable ways. This is a universal truth that applies to all human beings. And if you know the specific thought sequence that is necessary to produce feelings of fear in any human being, you will always know exactly why you (or others) have become afraid, whether you are consciously aware of such internal thought sequences or not.

This key principle explains why so many people who suffer from anxiety problems are perplexed about why these recurring "attacks" keep happening to them. It's bad enough that you may be having horrible feelings of panic and anxiety. But if you don't clearly understanding why this is happening to you, this uncertainty just adds additional layers of distress and suffering to your plight.

Yet the reason why you feel so afraid is very simple to understand. If you are feeling afraid, or if you are having full-blown panic attacks, you must be thinking, either consciously or unconsciously, in very specific ways that can be determined in advance and known with certainty.

The Internal Causes Of Fear In Human Beings

The internal causes (thoughts) that produce human fears are not complex, nor are they difficult to understand. You don't have to be a psychiatrist or a psychologist to appreciate them. It's just that this important knowledge hasn't been widely communicated, and therefore most people are still in the dark about it.

I'm now going to share with you this fear-producing sequence of thoughts, and when I do, you'll recognize them immediately. You will also easily recognize that they are indeed the thoughts, in a very general sense, that make you feel afraid and that also cause your panic attacks to escalate wildly.

Fear-Producing Thoughts

Something bad might happen (to me or to someone or something I care about).

Someone or something (including myself) might be hurt or harmed.

I don't have the power (control) to keep #1 or #2 from happening.

I should never feel afraid, since fear is a sign of weakness.

As I said, none of these internal causes of fear are difficult to comprehend. But without them being present, either consciously or unconsciously, you cannot feel afraid.

Let's see how this plays out with one very typical example of a panic attack.

-If you start to panic and your heart begins to race and you also begin to feel lightheaded, aren't you going to be thinking that something bad might happen?

-Aren't you going to conclude that you could become hurt or harmed?

-And since you didn't voluntarily cause these physical sensations to happen in the first place, isn't it likely you'll assume that you may not be able to stop them or keep them from causing you to have a heart attack, a stroke, etc.?

-And doesn't feeling afraid of these things make you feel ashamed and make you feel weaker than other people you might know?

So, understanding this specific thought sequence helps you to better understand why your feelings of intense fear and panic begin to escalate so quickly.

But what caused you to become fearful in the first place? What caused your heart to begin racing and your lightheaded feelings to emerge?

Well, if these are coming from fear, they have to be activated by the exact same thought sequence that causes your panic to intensify. In some form or another, you must have been either consciously or unconsciously having the very same thoughts, possibly without even knowing it, else it would be impossible to have become afraid in the first place.

Maybe you had a fearful thought or memory that you can't consciously recall. Maybe something happened to you, or around you, or to someone you care about that triggered your initial feelings of fear in the first place. All we know is that once the fear got started, it took off like a speeding train and kept building to greater heights of intensity.

But we do know that if you were feeling afraid (for whatever reason) you had to be thinking in exactly the fear-producing ways described above.

This is the first thing about fear and panic that you'll want to understand to eventually be able to get rid of this problem for good.

Here are two other very important things to know about fear, which also can help you to understand this emotion more accurately.

First, fear is what I call a "forward-looking" emotion. Many other common human emotions, such as anger, guilt, and frustration, are "backwards-looking" emotions. In other words, somebody (or you) did something a short time ago and when you think about it now, you start feeling angry or you begin to feel guilty. But the important thing to notice is that whenever you are angry or guilty, whatever you are feeling upset about is now in the past.

To the contrary, whenever you are feeling anxious or fearful, the thing you are feeling anxious about hasn't actually happened yet. Fear is an anticipatory human emotion, based more on your predictions of future events than actual events that either have or necessarily will occur.

The second key point about fear, which also relates to its anticipatory nature, is that your internal thoughts and predictions often turn out not to be true. I'm sure you've experienced this yourself, over and over again. But it's interesting that this important point about fear is almost always forgotten when you are having a panic attack.

It's very easy to demonstrate this key principle. Imagine you're getting ready to go to bed one night and as you enter your bedroom, you see a huge, brown, hairy-looking spider sitting right in the middle of your pillow. If you are like most people, you are likely to be startled by this observation and might instantly feel afraid.

Why did this fear reaction occur so instantaneously? Well, your body had to become triggered to think in our now known fear-producing ways. You had to be thinking like this:

Fear-Producing Thoughts

Something bad might happen. ("The spider might bite me.")

Someone or something (including myself) might be hurt or harmed. ("I could get poisoned or possibly even die.")

I don't have the power (control) to keep #1 or #2 from happening. ("Once I go to sleep, or if the spider runs away, I might not know if it returns and might not be able to protect myself.")

I should never feel afraid, since fear is a sign of weakness. (NOTE: this thought may not always be involved with every type of fear.)

So far, so good, yes? But what if someone in your family played a trick on you that night by placing a plastic (but realistic looking) spider on your pillow before you went to bed? What does this new knowledge reveal to you about your previous automatic fear-producing thoughts?

Is it true now that the spider can really hurt you? Is it true that you could suffer some type of pain, poisoning, or other physical harm? Is it true that you might not be able to protect yourself?

In retrospect, none of these original predictions were true at all. But when you (i.e. your body) automatically assumed they were all true, even though they weren't, your fear reaction occurred just as strongly as if you were dealing with a real, live, potentially harmful spider.

This may seem like a far-fetched example, but it's not. Because many of the fears that we have, about many different things, are also regularly caused by automatic thoughts that are just as false and just as mistaken as the ones in the plastic spider example above.

Step 2. Understanding Triggering and Automaticity

To truly appreciate how your emotions occur, here are two important concepts that are essential: Triggering and Automaticity. If you understand these two key aspects of how our bodies work, it will help you to better understand your panic attacks immensely.

As we grow and live our lives, our bodies become conditioned to respond in many automatic ways. If you are ticklish, for example, when someone playfully tickles you, your body may respond in one of several automatic ways—you might giggle, you might quickly withdraw from the touch, you might get angry, etc.

Whatever your particular response pattern might be, it likely happens automatically. This means you didn't try to respond in that way, you didn't think of it or will it, you didn't plan it—it just happened automatically, because that's how your body has become conditioned to respond.

Another good example is the classic knee-jerk reflex which most people are familiar with. Here, someone (usually a doctor) uses a small rubber hammer to tap very lightly on a spot just below your kneecap, when you are sitting with your legs flexed in a bent, relaxed position. For most people (but not all), this typically produces an automatic "knee-jerk" response, where their leg jumps out immediately. Here again, this is not a planned or willed response. It is simply a by-product of how most people's bodies are designed to automatically function.

In both examples, we could say that the tickle or the hammer tap was just a "trigger" and the response which resulted was our body's automatic way of responding—i.e. our "automaticity".

In the knee-jerk example, the response is usually the same for everyone. However, with the tickling example, each person's automatic response can be very different. How each person's body automatically responds to being tickled (including those who do not respond at all) will vary based on their own past history and previous encounters with being tickled.

Now why are the concepts of triggering and automaticity so important? How can they help you better understand your panic attacks?

Well, almost all of our emotions and other body reactions happen automatically—in response to external or internal triggering events. For example:

Somebody looks at you the wrong way and you automatically get angry.

Somebody points a loaded gun at you and you immediately become afraid.

Somebody suddenly accuses you of committing a serious misdeed and you automatically feel defensive, angry, or guilty.

These are all examples of external triggering events. However, your emotions can also result from internal triggering events.

For example, if you tell yourself, over and over again, that you are a terrible, unlovable person, this will probably trigger you to have some type of negative mood or emotion. It could be sadness, it could be disgust, it could be depression, it could be hopelessness, etc. But whatever it is, it originated from an internal triggering event within you.

Internal triggers can sometimes be conscious thoughts, like in the example above, or they can sometimes be perceived body sensations. So, for example, if your heart suddenly starts racing, this can be an internal trigger. If you suddenly experience a pain in your lower abdomen or start bleeding, both of these internal events will likely trigger some type of automatic responses in your mind and in your body.

So if you suffer frequently from panic attacks, it's important to remember two key things about triggering and automaticity:

Most of the emotions and other body sensations which occur during your attacks happen automatically. In other words, you don't CHOOSE to react with fear, or with rapid breathing or a rapid heart rate. These things just happen in your body automatically.

Second, how you automatically respond to certain internal or external triggers may be different from how other people respond to the exact same triggering events. Thus, you may have a panic attack in response to certain triggers where other people will not.

Now, how can this knowledge about triggering and automaticity help you with your panic attacks?

First, it helps you understand that when you go into panic mode, this is an automatic response pattern of your body. Thus, something had to trigger it! As you learned about the internal causes of fear in Step 1, you now know exactly what these triggers had to be. Somehow, whether you understand why or not, your body was triggered to think and believe the specific thoughts that must be present for the emotion of fear to occur.

Second, the internal thoughts that trigger your panic attacks may not always be thoughts you are consciously aware of. They can be unconscious thoughts you might have no way of detecting. However, you always know one thing for certain—if you are feeling afraid, those exact fear-producing thoughts must have become activated within you, whether you are aware of them or not. And now, as a result of reading this guide, you know exactly what these specific thoughts have to be.

And third, since all of this activity in your body and your mind (that's causing your panic to occur) is happening automatically, there's little you can do to stop it, control it, or even prevent it from occurring in the first place. As you probably know by now, it has a life of its own.

Thus, you are not a failure or a weak person because you can't keep your panic attacks from occurring. Just like you can't stop being ticklish (if you are) and you can't stop your leg from jerking when someone taps your kneecap in just the right place. These are automatic responses of your body which you cannot directly control.

However, with regard to panic attacks, even though you can't magically prevent them from happening or force them to stop immediately, you definitely can learn how to influence them once they get triggered within you.

This is the goal of the last three action steps in your 6-step plan, which I'm going to share with you shortly. But before we go there, there's one more key concept I think you might like to be clear about.

Step 3. Understanding The Double Whammy Effect

Full-blown panic attacks usually result from a "double whammy" effect that suddenly hits you. This "double whammy" is similar to getting hit by a "one-two punch" in boxing.

With panic attacks, first one thing hits you, and then before you can recover from that initial blow, another one hits you even harder. The combination of the two blows, which come very close together, can often be devastating.

The first blow is usually something that triggers you to get anxious in the first place. As we saw above, this can be an external event, a fearful circumstance, a conscious thought, an unconscious thought, or a fear-producing body sensation.

This is the spark that gets the panic attack rolling. This is the initial automatic fear trigger that causes physical fear responses to become activated within your body.

As a result of this initial fear response, your heart may start beating faster and you may become lightheaded, dizzy, or short of breath. Your vision may become distorted, your mind may start racing...you know the drill.

Now here's where the second blow comes in...hard.

As a result of the first automatic fear response, which came from whatever triggers might have started it, the physical fear sensations that also got triggered in your body now become a whole new set of triggers that result in a whole new set of fears!

Now, because your heart is racing, or because you're starting to feel lightheaded, etc., a second set of fear-producing thoughts gets activated within you. Whether these thoughts are conscious or unconscious, they usually are like this:

"Oh my god, something terrible is happening to me."

"I'm not going to be able to breathe."

"My heart is going to stop beating or I'm going to have a heart attack or stroke."

"I'm going to pass out, right here in front of everyone."

"I'm going to pee or crap my pants."

"I'm not going to be able to control my mind or my body."

Now, guess what happens when you automatically start having these types of fear-producing thoughts? That's right, you generate additional levels of fear and terror, and along with these come further, more intense physical sensations within your body.

And what do these more intense physical sensations do? They just escalate your initial set of fears about your health and make you feel even more scared and out of control.

So the double whammy concept doesn't even capture the whole story. Sometimes it can be a triple whammy or even a quadruple whammy, or more!

You see, once you've had your first panic attack, when the next one starts to occur, you are much more sensitive to being scared by it. And the more scared you are, the more physical symptoms of fear you're going to experience. And the more you experience physical symptoms of fear, the more you become fearful that your health or social standing is now at risk, even though they probably aren't.

So, the key understanding to take away from this third step is that panic attacks are not just one big upsetting event. They are composite events that always have multiple causes and reactions.

There's always an initial cause or triggering event, but you might not always be aware of what this is. The result of this initial trigger is your automatic fear response. But this initial physical response now becomes a new and second trigger, which produces additional fear-generating thoughts and fear responses, which then become a third set of fear triggers, and so on.

So this explains why panic attacks occur in the first place, and it also explains why they become so much more intense in a very short period of time. It's not really a mystery, and it also doesn't mean there is anything seriously wrong with you.

All it means is that you have a very strong propensity to become afraid (and to automatically think in ways that make you afraid). And when you do become afraid, you may not always apply the very best strategies for dealing with all the many automatic triggers, thoughts, and body responses going on.

And if you don't have well-developed skills (yet) for handling these multiple aspects of your panic attacks, you're going to feel more out of control...and hence more fearful.

However, once you learn how to respond to your panic attacks more expertly, and begin to have some initial success in doing so, your confidence will slowly build and you'll eventually discover that you do have a good deal of control over them. You might even find that you can make your panic attacks stop entirely...or almost entirely.

Remember, the type of control you actually do have is very different from the type of control you've been trying to exert over your panic attacks. As I've already said in this guide, you can't really do much to prevent your attacks from starting in the first place. And once they get rolling, you really can't do much to directly stop or control them very easily.

This doesn't mean, however, that you are out of options entirely. In fact, the options you do have are actually much more powerful, once you know how to use them properly.

That's what the last three steps in this 6-step method are designed to help you do. So now that you've got a much better background of understanding about your panic attacks, and why they keep happening to you, let's take a look at what you can do about them.

Chapter 7 Exercises To Help You Feel Better When

Depression Strikes

Depression will change the way you view life in almost every perspective. It causes mental and physical fatigue that interferes with your social and professional existence. Depression is not something anyone wants to endure. It contributes tremendously to low self-esteem, diminished health and happiness as a whole.

- Do you dread waking up in the mornings?

- Do you dread spending days alone?

- Are you tired of feeling lonely and depressed?

- Do you experience frequent headaches and don't know why?

- Are you afraid to express yourself because you feel that you have no valuable contribution to offer?

- Is your life different and less fulfilled than it once was?

- Are you having difficulty eating or tolerating your favorite foods?

- Do you separate yourself from others because you feel different or ashamed about something?

If your answers to three or more of the above questions are yes, you need to take proactive steps to battle and defeat depression. It can consume your life, but only if you allow it to do so.

Daily Steps

	Morning	Noon	Evening
Monday	Meditation	Have lunch outside	Paint or draw a picture
Tuesday	Yoga	Visit a new restaurant for lunch	Create a playlist
Wednesday	Morning Walk	Take an afternoon walk	Listen to your playlist
Thursday	Coffee with a Friend	Go to a museum	Rearrange a space in your home
Friday	Dance in the Mirror	Take a friend to lunch	Take a different route home
Saturday	Go Thrifting	Treat yourself to a spa day (nails, hair, massage)	Go out with friends
Sunday	Declare Affirmations	Bake a dessert for dinner	Take an evening stroll

*It is important that you take the necessary steps daily to defeat depression or to reduce the impact that it has on your life.

Daily Defeat of Negativity

The process to defeat negativity is one that must be repeated daily. Repetition is a staple for consistency in life. Begin each day by doing the following things.

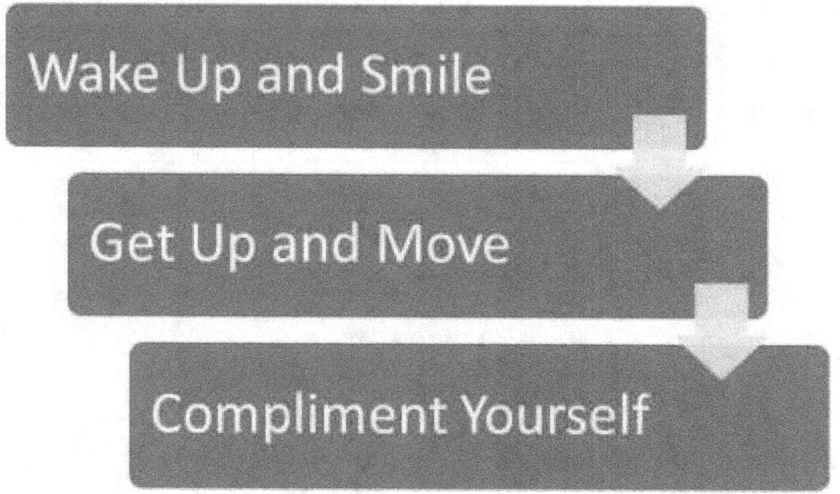

1. Wake Up and Smile – doing this sets the tone for your mood. It is important that you wake up feeling positive or you will succumb to the first negative encounter you have.

2. Get Up and Move – don't lounge around in the bed for too long after you awake. Remaining in bed gives you a moment to consider all that you must face and those things that brings sadness upon you. Once you get up, get moving.

3. Compliment Yourself – say something nice about yourself to enhance your mood or make you feel good. You should give yourself the first compliment of the day and carry yourself proudly wherever you go.

Self-Esteem Booster Cycle

You must create a cycle to boost your self-esteem. It is a never-ending cycle that keeps going and going. Whenever you feel down or defeated, repeat the words in the cycle. These are words of power and affirm the beliefs you should have about yourself.

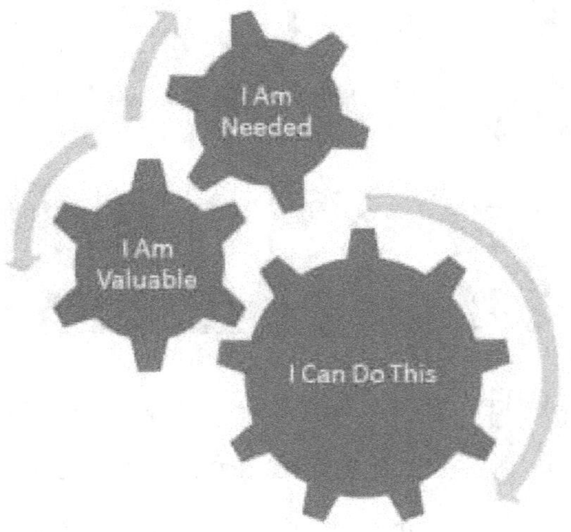

The Lifestyle Enhancer

Your lifestyle will be greatly enhanced when positive things and acts are introduced into it. Think positively. Speak positively. Believe positively. Act positively. This assist you in doing what is necessary to enjoy a positive lifestyle without room or time for depression.

Replace all negative words and thoughts with all things positive. This is a necessary component of the healing process when depression strikes. Your life has purpose but you must live and believe this to be true.

Below is a cycle of positivity to help enhance your lifestyle. Familiarize yourself with the cycle and incorporate it into your daily style of living.

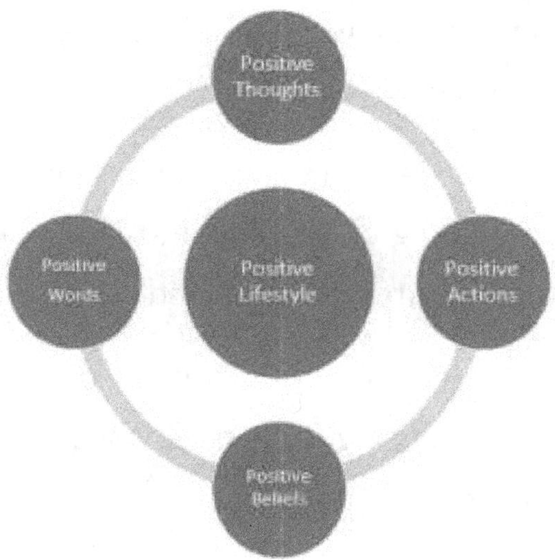

The Color Effect

The color effect is the process of exposing yourself to certain colors to help elevate or improve your mood. This is a positive channel in overcoming or defeating depression. It's not suggested that you decorate your living space in these colors only but to have them readily available in the moments you feel depressed.

The following colors have positive effects on your mood.

Blue is a color that is related to calmness. It helps you to feel relaxed and calm. The color also aides in decreasing blood pressure and producing clarity in the mind. Blue hues should be warm and not pastel to battle depression.

Yellow is a mood enhancing and invigorating color that energizes. Good energy is essential, as you attempt to battle depression. Embrace the color yellow in the early morning to set your mood for the day.

Green calms your anxiety and gives you a sense of reassurance about whatever is going on in your life. This color encourages tranquility. It also restores the mind and

Orange creates excitement and is great in motivating exercise. It's an upbeat color, so only focus on it when trying to get your energy levels up and not settle down.

Pink may not be a color that comes to mind when thinking of ways to enhance or improve your mood but it's a great one to do so. Exposure to this color settles the nerves and removes anxiety, anger and feelings of hostility.

Chapter 8 Avoiding Caffeine

While this section looks at which supplements work well for reducing anxiety, an important thing to remember is there are some things you take that may have a negative impact on your anxiety.

Really annoyingly for me, caffeine turned out to be a big trigger of anxiety for me. And I learned that it's a very common trigger for inducing anxiety and panic attacks.

How Do I Know If Caffeine Is Making My Anxiety Worse?

I love coffee. I have for years. I love the smell, I love the complexity of the flavor and I loved the way it woke me up in the mornings. For the past few years, my morning always started with a cup of good coffee and I'd sometimes have double espresso later on in the day if I needed an extra boost.

When I started having issues with anxiety and panic attacks, I read everything I could and learned there is a lot of evidence to suggest that caffeine can increase and sometimes even cause anxiety.

I obviously thought I was one of the lucky ones where that wasn't an issue, because I'd been drinking it long before any of these issues had occurred, so it couldn't have been the cause. I was obviously OK with caffeine... but after a couple of months of panic attacks and sustained anxiety, I decided to try cutting out caffeine for a couple of days to see if it made any difference — desperate times call for desperate measures.

On the first day, I had no coffee to start my morning. It was a bit more difficult to get going and I certainly yawned a few more times than I normally would have, but... I had no panic attacks and little to no anxiety.

Interesting.

So the next day, the same thing: no coffee and no anxiety.

On the third day, I decided to have my morning fix of caffeine again. It was delicious. I missed it. I missed the smell. I missed the taste. What I had not been missing was the anxiety and subsequent panic attack I had that morning.

Now I know that could have been a fluke. Correlation does not necessarily equate to causation. So I tried extending the "No Caffeine" experiment to two full weeks. During that time, I had no further issues with panic attacks and dramatically reduced ongoing anxiety.

At the end of the two weeks, I rewarded myself with a coffee... you can probably guess the experience. Anxiety increased and I had a panic attack within a couple of hours of drinking my cup of wonderful coffee.

I've since done my best to abstain from large doses of caffeine and it's certainly been a big driver in my reduced anxiety. Annoyingly, everything out there seems to have caffeine: headache medicine, soda drinks, even tea. Seemingly though, tea doesn't have a negative effect. I'm guessing it's due to the reduced caffeine content compared to coffee and the additional calming compounds like Theanine.

Giving Up Caffeine

Now you might be thinking, "Wow, I'd better give up caffeine right away!" There's a greater likelihood that you're thinking, "There's no way I'm giving up caffeine! It can't be bad for me. I've been drinking it for years! How am I going to get through my morning without that? I'll fall asleep at my desk!..." and so on.

Now look, I won't sugar-coat it. Going cold turkey on caffeine is up there with some of the more unpleasant experiences of my life and I would certainly like to avoid doing it again if possible. I had headaches, I felt tired, I was miserable... but I didn't have any panic attacks, so overall it was a plus.

The good news is that you can reap all the benefits of giving up caffeine cold turkey with none of the downsides. All you have to do is cut down gradually.

The plan

Before you go through any of this plan, first just try a day without caffeine. That's no coffee, no tea, no soda, no energy drinks or anything else with caffeine hidden in it. If you see an improvement in your symptoms or you feel any positive benefit at all, you owe it to yourself to try and wean yourself off caffeine, even if it's only for a short time.

It's simple really. All you need to do is lower your intake of daily caffeine, a little bit at a time, over the course of a week or two.

Here, I'm going to use coffee as an example as it tends to be the most prominent source of caffeine for many people.

•	Day 1: Just drink your normal amount of coffee.

•	Days 2 – 5: Start blending your coffee with around 50% decaffeinated. Continue to drink that until the end of day 5.

•	Day 6: Next, blend 25% of your regular coffee with 75% decaf for one day.

•	Day 7: Drink only decaf coffee.

CONGRATULATIONS! You're now officially off coffee!

Now if you go through that and don't see any improvement, you're one of the lucky ones who can have caffeine without issue! Grab a cup of Joe and enjoy your morning.

If, however, you're like me or the majority of people experiencing anxiety, you'll probably have seen a marked improvement by cutting out caffeine. If that's the case, it's easier than you think to live without caffeine.

How to live without caffeine

There are a few different options to replace caffeinated drinks with to help you stick to your plan.

• Caffeine-free soft drink – They are pretty easy to find if you read the labels.

• Sparkling water – It's an acquired taste, but it's the most amazing thing! They make some naturally flavored with fruit juice and things, too.

• Decaf coffee – If you get the good brands, it tastes the same! And you can enjoy one later in the evening without it screwing with your sleep.

The only thing I haven't found a good substitute for energy drinks yet. They're basically just caffeine drinks so stick to sparkling water if you can. If not, a caffeine-free soft drink if you need that sweetness or fruit juice flavored sparkling drinks work well, too.

Other Benefits of Eliminating Caffeine

So you're still weighing whether to cut out caffeine or not. I get it. It's a hard thing to considered because it's so engrained in all of our lives.

If the thought of potentially eliminating your anxiety over-night isn't enough of a driver for you, there are a few other reasons you should consider eliminating caffeine.

Save money

> That daily coffee can add up and thousands of dollars a year.

- A Grande Starbucks Latte: $3.65 a day | $26 a week | $1,332 a year

- 5-hour energy: $3 a day | $21 a week | $1,095 a year

- Home brewed coffee: $.71 a day | $5 per week | $259 a year

- Monster Energy Drink: $3 a day | $21 a week | $1,095 a year

- K-cups: $.65 a day | $4.55 a week | $237 a year

> That's some pretty serious savings. Just think what you could do with that extra couple of grand a year!

Lower your blood pressure

> Caffeine has been shown to raise your blood pressure. Cutting out caffeine can lower your blood pressure and keep your heart healthier for longer.

Better sleep

> Caffeine can have a large, detrimental impact on the quality of your sleep. Drinking coffee or other caffeinated drinks too late in the day can interfere with getting to sleep as caffeine tends to stay in your system for four to six hours.

A good idea is to at least cut out caffeine after 12 noon and you should see a marked improvement in the quality of your sleep.

Better mood

Caffeine alters your mood. It's not uncommon to hear people say they're grumpy until they've had their morning coffee and they start to feel lethargic when it starts to wear off in the afternoon.

If you quit caffeine altogether, you no longer have these ups and downs. You can have sustained energy throughout the day with no crashes and no grumpiness.

Whiter and healthier teeth

It's well known that coffee and tea can stain your teeth. Energy drinks and soft drinks are just as bad and they can erode tooth enamel and can cause decay.

Eliminating them will help you towards healthier and (some would say, more importantly) whiter teeth.

Significant weight loss

Caffeinated drinks generally add empty calories to our diets that don't benefit us in any way. Many experts state that sugary beverages are a large factor in the obesity epidemic .

Look at what you could save by cutting out those caffeinated drinks.

• Quitting a "one energy drink per day" habit saves 200 calories per day, 1,400 calories a week, and 73,000 calories a year!

• Quitting that "one Starbucks Vanilla Latte per day" would save you 250 calories per day, 1,750 calories a week, and 91,250 calories a year!

Are you kidding me? Over 90,000 calories a year? Here's a simple tag-line: "Cut out your vanilla Latte and get abs."

No more jitters

One of the main side-effects people experience with caffeine is jittery or shaky hands. This could be a minor inconvenience, or a major one. Either way, quitting can steady your steady hands again and steady your progress toward a healthier self.

Lower risk of cardiac issues

Caffeine stimulates the heart muscles, causing your heart to beat with more powerful contractions. Those with underlying heart conditions can be at risk. Remember, too, that a stronger push by the muscles could relate to increased interior vessel pressures and weakening of the blood vessel walls.

Reduced risk of Type 2 Diabetes

Black coffee can actually reduce the risk of diabetes. Unfortunately, most people don't drink plain black coffee. Sugared coffee or caffeinated beverages can actually increase your risk of diabetes by up to 26%, according to the Harvard School of Public Health.

So as you can see, there are a number of benefits for cutting out caffeine. It doesn't have to be permanent and with the Easy Quit Plan, it doesn't even have to be hard. Try it — you owe it to yourself!

Chapter 9 You Can Heal From Anxiety Disorder

It is completely possible to heal yourself from anxiety disorder. As already mentioned briefly, anxiety is an apprehensive state of mind that comes about from thinking something might be harmful or dangerous. An example of this would be hearing a noise that sounds like someone might be trying to break into your house. This will result in anxiety if you think the other person is threatening to your life or situation. Thus, anxiety happens once you start thinking and acting in apprehensive ways, or imagining and thinking that there is something that will cause us harm.

Imagination's Role in Anxiety:

It helps to notice here that anxiety comes from thinking about, or imagining, some circumstance or situation that is impending that might hurt us in some way. Therefore, anxiety comes from the methods we use to cope with the ideas of risk, uncertainty, or future problems. The symptoms of anxiety are, in fact, stress symptoms. They are called symptoms of anxiety since acting overly hesitant or apprehensive causes too much stress, and thus, symptoms. This means there are two parts of the process of anxiety:

- Your own Thoughts and Behavior: The first component involves the way you act and think. This is the first step to anxiety or panic, which then will lead to...

- Physical Symptoms: These thoughts you have cue the symptoms of anxiety including the racing heart, obsessive thoughts, and sweaty palms. You might feel as though you're going to be sick, pass out, or start shaking violently. Oftentimes, the fear of these symptoms is worse than the symptoms themselves and makes them worse.

Acting anxious leads to this physical reaction in your body, each and every time, whether you are aware of it or not. How much of a physical reaction there is results directly from how much anxious behavior there are? In other words, the more anxiety you feel, the more intense your reaction will be physically. This means that to get past anxiety problems, you have to recognize and respond to the reasons you feel so apprehensive in the first place. These reasons can be thought of as the underlying reasons for your anxiety.

The Formula for Overcoming Anxiety:

When you figure out and address the reasons you have for behaving and thinking like an anxious person, you can eliminate and reduce this behavior. As soon as you can eliminate this type of behavior, and teach your body to stop being over-stressed and anxious, your body will stop exhibiting these harmful stress symptoms.

- Recognize and Address: The first step is to identify the reasons that you have this anxiety trigger, and then address them. You can then replace these behaviors with healthier coping methods for risk and uncertainty. For instance, maybe you have anxiety about being in social situations that you haven't properly looked at yet. Maybe you were in a situation where you got called out in front of a lot of people and got embarrassed, and ever since then, you are afraid to put yourself out there in any social environment. Tracing back your anxieties to their origins can help you to move past them.

- The "Worst Case" Scenario: What is it that you actually fear? Is it that people will laugh at you? What will happen after that? These are the questions you have to start asking yourself to get to the root of your anxiety, instead of latching onto avoidance. Oftentimes, you'll realize that your worst fear is something you'd quickly get over. It might also help to recall other times when you encountered hardships and what happened as a result. Chances are, you recovered and even learned a few things along the way. This is helpful to look at because it puts your fears and anxiety into perspective.

- Stress gets Reduced: Doing the above step will result in relief from stress for your body and a calmer state of mind. Then, your body will stop producing the symptoms through repeating those steps. This method, used in conjunction with some of the other tips in the book, will help you get your anxiety disorder under control.

- Self-Fueling Cycle: Following these steps will then create a new cycle. Rather than a cycle of anxiety and torment, you can create a new pattern of calm. Our minds respond to repetition, which then forms new habits. In order for this to stick, you have to repeat it tirelessly until your anxiety and worry begins to loosen its hold on your mind and life. It's time to learn the different ways that you are being held back by this disorder and commit to changing them and improving your life and health.

Consider this, you were not born anxious. None of us were because that is not our natural state. You picked up behaving in an apprehensive and anxious way along the route of your life, either from how you were raised, or experiences you had that brought you to certain conclusions. Therefore, you can teach yourself alternative methods for handling risk and uncertainty. This is simply a matter of replacing your current responses with calmer ones. Does this happen right away? No, but it will change if you stick with it and keep trying. Let's look at another level of this problem.

Neuroplasticity and Anxiety:

Since the human brain can change the way it functions (through something called neuroplasticity), you can change your patterns and habits of thought. The trick is repetitive action or thought, which then becomes a new habit over time. Now, this doesn't happen immediately, just as your current way of anxious thinking didn't happen right away. You've been practicing this for a long time, and it may take a while of practicing the new way before it sticks, so don't get discouraged. Anyone can heal their own anxiety. The human brain is always capable of making healthy changes, meaning that you are not doomed to feel anxious forever. This is only the first step to healing this problem, and we will offer you many more throughout the course of this guide.

Chapter 10 Love Yourself

What is Self-Love?

Self-love means showing compassion to ourselves. You are not to be harsh with yourself and criticize every single thing. We often tend to do that when things don't go quite our way. Every time someone does a task better than us, we often blame ourselves for simply not being perfect.

A human being is made to make mistakes. But berating yourself on them relentlessly can cause serious damage to your self-esteem. The lower your self-esteem goes, the more likely you are to fall into depression and anxiety.

Practicing self-love techniques builds greater self-esteem. Better self-esteem is directly linked to good mental health. Self-compassion brings about these constructive habits.

Optimistic nature.

Lesser depression.

Lesser anxiety.

Putting the stress behind oneself.

We have to realize that mistakes and struggles are part of life. Those imperfections are what reality is. Self-love has some aspects to it, which are:

Humanity: To know you are just human and can make mistakes, but they don't define you.

Kindness: Like you treat the people around you with generosity. Self-kindness means also diverting some of that tenderness to yourself.

Self-love will give you hope and will help you pursue healthy behaviors in life.

Self-Compassion

Some simple steps for self-compassion are as below:

Recognize when you are giving into a negative state of mind. If anxiety starts to creep up, then it is time to call it out. Acknowledge that these feelings are affecting you. It's better to accept than shut it out completely.

Imagine if your loved one was going through the same thing, what would your reaction be. It won't be harsh and criticizing, will it? You will be kind and caring because you know they don't deserve it.

Rather than blaming yourself for your behavior, try to find an explanation for it and don't judge yourself immediately. Everything is not always black and white. It is our anxiety that tends to make us feel vulnerable and not be comfortable with ourselves and our thoughts. Making mistakes is common, but accepting them and promising to yourself to change for the better, is what real growth is as a person.

We often categorize ourselves to the lowest of the low and put others on the highest stage where they are practically flawless, which, in fact, is not true at all. Most successful people have owned to making great blunders. What they didn't do afterward is let those shortcomings of theirs to put a damper on their accomplishments. They believed in themselves and carried on.

If you have done something horrid, you feel responsible for, then it is not healthy to wallow in it forever. At some point, you have got to get up and think about what can be done to make amends. Those who love will support you, but ultimately it is up to you to make changes for the sake of yourself. You have to take the reins of your own life.

Self-love and Anxiety Disorders

Self-love is being patient and amiable towards yourself so that you can develop healthy habits essential for wellbeing. To find inner peace, it is necessary to practice loving yourself. When you truly love yourself, you can achieve true happiness. How can you be truly happy when on the inside you don't accept yourself?

Loving yourself is not to be translated into egoistic behavior. It is definitely not narcissism. Self-love doesn't mean you stop caring about values and do what you constantly want because that is what makes you happy. It is not built on the feeling of jealousy and envy. Those green monsters are opposite to self-care.

It is a feeling of being worthy of happiness. No matter what you do, you cannot escape your body. So, it is better not to make it a prison for yourself. By being honest, accepting, and respectable towards yourself, you are truly allowing yourself to evolve into a better version.

If you don't love yourself how can you extend that feeling towards others?

Techniques of self-love for anxiety

Self-love helps in the portrayal of how you behave and defines your personality. Self-love promotes self-confidence. It can lead you to succeed at work and in your social life. It is one of the best weapons against anxiety. By regularly practicing self-love, you are sure to lead an anxiety free life. Self-love will readily prompt you to make healthier life changes. So, by design, a healthy lifestyle keeps you away from anxiety and stress.

Most sensitive people are often prone to anxiety. Realizing that you are not what you feel is the first step to heal. If you feel overwhelmed, then this realization can give you a clear perspective and help you get rid of that feeling.

Get to know yourself better and don't be swayed easily by others' opinions of you. People who have self-love don't act in accordance to what others want. If you are in tune with your inner self, you will automatically experience less anxiety.

Surround yourself with people who truly care about your wellbeing. If you realize someone is detrimental for your mental health, then there is no shame in cutting away from that relationship. If you have a positive environment around you, it will help you more with your anxiety.

Practice conscious breathing. As soon as you feel like stress is going to get you and you will get a panic attack, talk positively to yourself. If you are facing a hectic schedule or any situation that makes you nervous, some positive self-talk is a great coping mechanism. Verbally outlay things you need to do and ensure yourself that you will get through it.

Indulge yourself in self-soothing habits, such as running a scented bath or using a calming scent in your house. Put on your favorite show. Get in the comfiest outfit that you can find. Seek warmth, sit by a cozy fireplace.

Enjoy some superfoods. They will impact your blood sugars and energy levels. It will help regulate those. Food impacts our brain and thus our mood also. Some of these superfoods are below.

Almonds

Chocolate

Berries

There is a phenomenon known as 'Biophilia.' It explains that humans feel calmer and stress-free in nature. So, try to connect with earth any way you can and you don't need to be a hiker or climber. You can tend to a small garden or visit the park, etc. Playing with sand also reduces stress so just build a sand castle at the beach.

Acupressure has been practiced throughout centuries and people have documented its advantages. There are two acupuncture points located between the skull and neck. They are said to help with stress and anxiety. This is what you need to do if you want to try it.

Place your thumbs at the top of the neck. It where the neck meets your skull

Apply gentle pressure.

The pressure must not be soft but firm. Keep pressing and throughout it slowly and deeply breathe three times.

After that lazily float your hands in your lap.

Then drop your chin to your chest slowly.

In the end, take a deep breath and smile to top it off.

You have to start with love to get away from negativity. Anxiety triggers negative emotions like a shame for not being able to do things, not being able to handle situations and having a constant fear of anxiety attack. Anxiety is a one step forward two step backward kind of thing. You must have loads of patience. This is real life, not a movie where a single moment tends to make everything better. It is a good place to start your journey, but the real deal is the ride to reach that finish line.

How not loving yourself causes anxiety

When you don't care about your wellbeing, then it is called self-abandonment. It is directly related to anxiety.

Emotional self-abandonment is when you deliberately don't pay attention to how anxiety is making you suffer inside out. Loving yourself emotionally means you have a strong inner bond in place. When things upset you, rather than feeling helpless, you work it out with yourself. Anxiety will struggle to get hold of you if you start to practice true self-love.

Physical self-abandonment happens when we let ourselves go and don't think what is healthy for us. We don't sleep enough, don't drink water enough, or have an unhealthy diet. All of these things, if not resolved, are a one-way ticket to anxiety kingdom. Loving yourself physically means taking care of your diet and health. Health is true wealth after all.

Financial self-abandonment means that either you overspend and regret afterward or you don't spend money at all not even for your basic needs. When you do spend, you want to get the cheapest thing for fulfilling your need. You are not enjoying yourself this way and it can lead to unhappiness. Troubles with money related to debt are one of the biggest causes of stress.

Organized self-abandonment means that your schedule is a mess. You are not organized in your daily life. Being a bit mature and adult-like is helpful. Being organized and following a schedule are keys to success and will make you less prone to anxiety.

Relationship self-abandonment means that in a relationship, it is important that you resolve conflict not by giving in and going along with whatever the other person wants. You have to make them see what you want and then you both have to work on it. If you are constantly putting yourself down just to please others, it will end up doing you and your relationship more harm than good.

Spiritual self-abandonment is when you don't ask your higher power for guidance, wisdom, and love then it is likely that you will end up feeling lonely and depressed. Loving yourself spiritually means to stay in contact with higher power and seek peace within, so you can efficiently fight off anxiety.

Disadvantages of Low Self-Esteem

Low self-esteem is generally caused by not giving any regard to yourself. Having low self-esteem is often linked to anxiety disorders.

Social anxiety disorder

If you have low self-esteem, you are more likely to develop a social anxiety disorder later on. Low self-esteem can make one feel lonely. It highlights more negative aspects of your image to yourself.

General anxiety disorder

General anxiety disorder is often linked to having low self-esteem. It is a feeling of being unworthy. Self-esteem of a person develops by how they view themselves based on others' reactions towards them. People who are showered with lots of affections by others tend to have high self-esteem. Those who are getting rejected don't have a lot of self-confidence. People with anxiety disorder experience more rejection from their surroundings; some of it is all in their heads though.

You should evaluate how much people stand by you and how much they neglect you. One important question is how much do they matter to you? If they don't matter to you, then their rejection doesn't hold a lot of meaning. If they are closer ones, then it is usually stress and anxiety that is pushing them away. Seeking therapy for GAD will help you improve your relationships.

People with anxiety and low self-esteem become stuck and inactive. They feel demoralized to perform an action because of all the negative reasons they have conjured in their mind. General anxiety disorder will hinder your ability to take action.

Remember to acknowledge your accomplishments and thinking back to them will give you motivation.

Advantages of self-love

As you get more confident in ourselves, you tend to delay tasks, less in favor of perfection, as you did before. You develop a go-getter attitude that helps you pursue talks more easily.

We don't let failure get us down. We know setbacks are not intended to be mulled over, but to learn from and move on.

We learn to not let criticism get to us. We acknowledge negative feedback, but we don't take it as a personal attack. We get to approach it with an open mind.

Treating Your Panic Attacks

Thankfully, this condition is treatable. It could be a combination of one or several treatments that get the job done, but the most important thing to remember is, help is available. It is possible to overcome the condition you're so afraid of, and if you don't want to rely on medication as the only tool for treating your panic attacks, there are other strategies available to you. Building a self-help strategy toolbox can prove to be a very effective way of coping with panic attacks and panic disorders, and ultimately overcome the anxiety you've fought against for so long. Before you begin, it probably feels like an impossible task you're about to undertake. But it only feels impossible because you haven't equipped yourself with the right tools yet.

What needs to be included in your toolbox of self-help strategies are:

- Knowledge - You need to know what you're up against and what you're dealing with. Knowledge gives you the power you need to understand what is happening to your body the moment you undergo a panic attack and why. With the information you gather from each episode, you're analyzing the triggers, and that is the first stepping stone to dealing with this condition. It is easy to live in fear and avoidance when you don't understand what is happening. Being afraid of the unknown is a natural response but getting trapped in a cycle of avoidance and living your life in fear is no way to live. Panic attacks are frightening, yes, but they are not as harmful as you might think once you begin working on overcoming your triggers. With knowledge, your goal is not to immediately eliminate your panic right then and there. What you're trying to do instead is understand what you're up against so you can better manage the way you feel without letting your fear take over.

- Breath Relaxation Techniques - Relaxation techniques should be a staple in any toolbox to overcome panic attacks and anxiety. Keeping your body calm and relaxing your muscles is the key to taking back control of the mind. When you're anxious, and in panic mode, your body seizes up. Your mind is racing, and the stress hormones pumping through your veins are not helping you see the situation any clearer. Calm breathing is one example of a necessary relaxation technique. When you're panicked, you're hyperventilating, also commonly referred to over-breathing. This is only further triggering your anxious emotions. You need to counter that with a breathing technique that helps you fight these symptoms and remain calm, despite what your body is trying to tell you. Calm breathing begins by inhaling slowly through your nose for four seconds. Hold that breathe for two seconds, and then exhale slowly through your mouth for four seconds. Wait two to three seconds in between breaths before you resume. This technique is meant to regulate the oxygen flow through your body to minimize the dizziness and lightheaded feeling which often ensues during moments of panic.

- Muscle Relaxation Techniques - Once you've got control of your breath, it's time to focus on the rest of your body. Equip your toolbox with muscle relaxation techniques that work for you. The purpose of these techniques is to minimize the muscular aches and pains you feel when you experience a panic attack. Tension in the muscles is often focused around the neck and shoulder areas in particular. You need to relax those muscles, and this practice can be done throughout the day whenever you feel that your body is too tense. It doesn't necessarily have to happen only when you're feeling panicked. Start by focusing on the specific muscle group, purposely tensing that targeted group for several seconds, breathing deeply while you hold the tension for five seconds, and then make a big effort to relax as you exhale your breath. Pause for 10 seconds or so, and then either repeat the same process on the same muscle group or move onto the next area you think needs it.

- Challenge Your Overestimation - Guessing, assuming, and anticipating what is going to happen is only feeding into your panic. The anxious mind tends to overestimate and predict the worst possible outcome without focusing on the facts the way they should be. Overcoming panic attacks means you need to go against this instinct to force yourself to focus on the evidence in front of you. Take each panicked thought you have and look for the supporting evidence? Is there enough to substantiate panic? How much of what you're thinking is overestimation? Do you often have similar thoughts during other panic attack episodes? Pushing back using the facts can be extremely helpful in slowing down the mind long enough to realize maybe you're overestimating and catastrophizing more than you should be.

- Create Coping Cards - Panic and anxiety can be tough to deal with, so any support or coping methods go a long way toward making a difference. Challenging your unhelpful thoughts in times of panic can be difficult, especially when you're alone with no immediate support system nearby. In that case, you need to make your own system. Like using coping cards to challenge your thinking. Take a couple of index cards and then write some realistic thoughts on each of these cards in big, bold letters. Carry these cards around with you throughout the day. Statements you can write on your cards include:

- I am capable of handling this.

- This moment will not last forever

- No one should dictate how anxious I feel

- Every problem has a solution

- I should check if I am confusing thoughts with facts

- Connecting Directly with Love and Support - Your friends and family are going to be your strongest support system in this phase of your journey. Panic attacks and anxiety can feel a lot worse when it feels like you're doing this alone. Isolation and loneliness can be a very lonely experience, and it is important now more than ever that you reach out to those you can count on.

Chapter 11 Diagnostic Physical Symptoms

Anxiety has the potential to have detrimental effects on an individual's body. These complications are very tricky during moments they become chronic. They have the potential of causing an individual to develop chronic conditions that affect his or her physical being. There are several types of research that have been made on anxiety. The focus made to discover what develops anxiety has taken the globe by utmost efforts. The research made by the medical community has seen some success in discovering the source. Their findings said that anxiety is developed in the brain. The specific part of the brain is known as the amygdala. The amygdala is the part of the brain that is responsible for managing all the emotional responses in an individual's life.

The brain is a complex part of the body. It sends the signals to rest of the body parts when some emotional responses are triggered. These emotional responses that the brain sends signals to other parts of the body include stress, fright, and anxiety. The signals that are sent by the mind to the body prepare an individual's body to prepare for a flight or fight. The body of an individual is meant to release cortisol which is described as the stress hormones

These hormones known as flight and fight are useful. They come with great help when an individual is dealing with danger ahead of him or her. However, there are moments when these hormones are of no use. Such situations include while taking tests or interviews. There levels where this response cannot be described as healthy or normal. Such instances include when these responses persist for a very long time or frequently.

There are several ways in which anxiety can affect a person's body. They include:

Breathing and Respiratory Changes

This is a common occurrence when individual experience anxiety attacks. The breathing of an individual can shift to being very shallow and rapid. This phenomenon is usually referred to as hyperventilation. The process makes a person have extreme difficulties handling his or her day to day activities. It is because the process of hyperventilation overstretches the working of an individual's lungs.

Hyperventilation gives the lungs an expanded role by allowing them to take more amounts of oxygen. It goes further to making the lungs supply these inhaled oxygen rapids to the body of an individual. The oxygen supplied in rapidly and in huge quantities has a specific role it plays. The oxygen aids a person's body to prepare for the flight or fight response. This phenomenon has the potential of making an individual feel like he or she is being deprived of oxygen. It makes an individual experience several sessions of gasping for breath. Therefore, it can worsen hyperventilation phenomenon. The common symptoms for hyperventilation include feeling faint, feeling weak, tingling effect and feeling dizzy.

Response by the Cardio Vascular System

Anxiety can cause some effects in an individual heart rate. The mental state shifts the normal palpitation of a person's heart. It goes beyond affecting the circulation of blood in an individual's body. Having a fast heart rate is very advantageous to individuals. It helps to overcome the state of flight and fight that is triggered by the mind. This process is possible because increased blood flow helps the muscles of a person to get fresh oxygen and nutrients.

Vasoconstriction has the potential of affecting an individual's body temperature. Vasoconstriction is described as the phenomenon by which the blood vessels narrow. Several people across the world have experienced some hot flashes. This is as a result of vasoconstriction. There are several responses an individual's body can use in order to control the situation. Most common phenomenon entails an individual's body sweating to cool down. Several people feel cold when the process is effective ongoing.

If the occurrence of anxiety is very detrimental when it persists for long. It affects the cardiovascular system of an individual and the general health of a person's heart. There are several scientific types of research that have been conducted on the effect of anxiety on an individual heart. These researches prove that a healthy person is predicted to be affected by heart conditions in moments he or she has persistent anxiety attacks.

Impaired Immune Function

Anxiety has the potential of boosting an individual's body immune response in a short time. On the other hand, persistent anxiety has the exact opposite effect of an individual's body. One of the flight or fight hormones that released known as cortisol is responsible for this effect. Cortisol hinders the release of a substance responsible for causing inflammation the body. This switches off the feature of the body immune system that is responsible for fighting infections. The occurrence impairs a person immune response. Therefore, people with anxiety disorders that are chronic are likely to have some infections. These infections include likes of common cold and flu.

Changes in the Digestive System

This point is also influenced by cortisol hormone. During the process of flight and fight, the body blocks some processes that it considers that they are not essential during these moments. The process of blocking process affects the process of digestion in a human being. The process is also hugely affected by the other form of hormones that are produced during the flight or fight sate. Adrenaline is what is being referred to. It makes an individual body to reduce the amount of blood flowing and it makes the muscles of the stomach to relax.

This causes several effects on an individual's body when he or she is experiencing anxiety attacks. An individual can experience diarrhea, nausea and the feeling of one's stomach-churning. A person can go to the extent of losing his or her appetite because of such occurrences in his or her body. There were some scientific researches that prove relationship between mental states and digestive system. It revealed that several mental states such as depression are linked up to diseases such as irritable bowel syndrome. A study was conducted in Mumbai India at a gastroenterology clinic. The findings of the research conducted revealed that about 30%-40% of the participants who had irritable bowel syndrome also suffered from anxiety.

Urinary Response

An individual experiencing anxiety attacks will have an increased urge to urinate every time. This kind of reaction is mostly associated with a common group people. The most affected people tend to be a group of people who have phobias. Phobia can be described as a situation where an individual is afraid of certain things even before they happen. The thought of these things happening to them causes an individual to experience anxiety attacks. An individual need to urinate every time or individual losing control over the process of urination may have some anchoring to an evolutionary base. It is because it is very easy for an individual to flee moments with anxiety with a bladder that it is empty. Moreover, there have been several scientific studies that have been conducted over years on the relationship between increased urge to urinate and anxiety. However, these researches have not been successful in linking up increased urge to urinate with anxiety attacks.

Stressful Situations that have Happen over Time

Everybody in the modern world has had situations where he or she experienced stress. However, there are certain situations in life that top when the issue concerning stress is raised in day to day life human beings. They include:

Death of a Loved One

When a spouse or a loved one occurs, it makes it one of the leading causes of stress in an individual's life. It is one of the most stressful things a person has to handle. The process of bereavement affects people in several ways because people are different. An individual is predicted to have several feelings at this point. He or she is predicted to either feel shocked, guilty or angered. The process may make one feel like his or her world has been distorted and turned to face upside down. It is because one is always in a state of limbo on how to handle life without these people present in their lives.

Therefore, it is important for an individual to learn how to take care of themselves during these situations. One of the best ways it can be done is by an individual trying to eat balanced diets and having enough rests. It is also great when one relies on other people for support instead of doing so much. It is good to talk out with family and friends who are close during such moments. It is because healing from such an incidence comes with an individual talking out and sharing his or her sentiments. The loss of a loved one has a very long journey when one needs healing. If an individual has difficult moments during handling of normal life situations, he or she is advised to seek professional help during such times.

Separation or Divorce

Divorce and separation of couples is also another leading form of stressful events in the globe. There are situations that partners sit down together and agree on the way to end their relationship. However, there are several issues that are emotional and practical during the process that can be emotionally draining during the process. These issues include child custody, living arrangement, and financial issues.

There are several things an individual can do to help him or herself to heal from the situation. The process of healing first starts with an individual surrounding oneself with a support system that is good. The next step involves an individual taking his or her time and staying fit physically. There are certain ways an individual can balance up the situation. He or she can stay civil to his or her partner and having honest talks with the kids about the whole process.

Getting Married

This is always one of the days individuals are happy because of it always one of the most awaited days. However, it has the potential of turning out to be one of the most stressful life events. Planning wedding and making it be successful can be one of the most stressful things around the world. There are various complexities that attach themselves to this event. An individual is always worried if his or her guests will have fun during the events. It becomes even more stressful for an individual when family conflicts arise during the day. This may make a big day feel more overwhelming to an individual.

There are several ways an individual can be able to keep the stress brought by planning the wedding. The first step entails keeping the communication channels open. An individual is supposed to be open in telling his or her family members on what he or she envisions for the day. The second step involves an individual being able to priorities things that are important to him or her. During all these processes, it very critical for an individual to be able to take care of him or herself. One is also supposed to keep an open communication channel with his or her partner.

Starting a New Job

There are several places an individual can start his or her career in the modern world. However, it is a cause of stress to several people across the globe. The reason behind this concept is that people tend to feel overwhelmed when he or she is being shown his or her new roles in the new workplace. It is a tense moment because there are new things and a new environment an individual will be experiencing.

There two things an individual is not supposed to be afraid of doing. The first is to ask questions about roles that are not clarified an instructor. The second thing includes not being afraid of seeking assistance on thinks you do not know because it is a new environment one is experiencing. Therefore, one is supposed to remember that he or she cannot be perfect on his or first day at work.

Work Place Stressors

One-quarter of the people who work tend to believe that the work they do is one of their biggest stressors. There are several issues that can affect an individual at work. These issues include handling the job for the first time, fear of getting sucked and heavy workloads. Other job stressors in the current world include poor work management and times when one does not have control over his activities at work. The stress creeping from work has the effect of influencing an individual's other sectors of life. If the situation is persistent, it has detrimental effect on an individual's health.

To cub this form of stress, there are simple ways an individual can use. He or she can start by making a specific time to efficiently work while on duty. He or she is supposed to go ahead and prioritizing the tasks he or she is handling at the place of work. It is also often helpful when an individual learns to delegate work when he or she is overwhelmed during certain situations. Some of this common phenomenon at the workplace that overwhelms people includes presentation of key business report in a meeting.

Financial Problems

This is also one of the leading causes of stress in the current world because of the tight economy. Recent research was conducted by the American Psychological Association. The research revealed that approximately 76% of the American believed that financial constraints were the major cause of stress. The recent world has seen several rise and fall in the economy. The presence of inflation and economic depressions give people a hectic time. They make money so hard to find through reduction of money supply. On the other hand, money can easily be available but commodities and services are very expensive.

After the research finding by the American Psychological Association, several recommendations were made to help people being stressed over finances. The remedy found involved an individual finding out which is his or her financial stressor and finding possible solution to overcome it. An individual was also advised to examine how he or she usually deals with financial stress. Unhealthy behaviors such as drinking and gambling are uncalled for as a means to relieve stress. The last recommendation entails encouraging an individual to use these financial stress periods as an accelerant to become better.

Chapter 12 Possible Causes Of Relationship Anxiety

The main cause of anxiety is the inner critical voice. This cause of anxiety borrows its ideas from our persona experiences; things we have experienced, lessons we learnt from others, comments we have heard other people making, et cetera. The things we were exposed to in our childhood years contribute a lot to our current perception of relationships. What gender stereotypic statements did you hear in your childhood from the people who had influence in your life? What was your understanding of love and relationships? How was your first relationship experience? These experiences infiltrate our viewpoints and cover our current perception.

Everyone has a different inner critic voice. However, some subjects cut across these thoughts

Avoiding relationships

- People who get into relationships just end up getting hurt

- Relationships never work out

- Everyone is getting a divorce

About a partner

- Men are so self-centered, insensitive and unreliable

- Women are so needy, clingy, expensive, and fragile

- He only cares about sex and staying with his friends,

- All she ever wants is to go shopping for expensive items.

- Why is he saying that he loves me? Is there a hidden agenda?

- You cannot trust anyone

- He/she cannot get anything right,

- He/she is probably a cheat

- If he/she is so good, why did the former partner leave him/her?

About self

- Do not get too attached to him/her

- You will never find a person who understands you

- Even the other partner left you

- Love is not for you,

- It is your fault if you lose him/her

- He/she is too good for you,

- You have to keep him/her interested; otherwise, he/she will leave

- As soon as he/she finds out the truth about you, he/she will leave.

- You are better off on your own

- Relationships are not your thing.

Chapter 13 The Benefits of Vagus Nerve Stimulation

Something I have seen time and time again, not only in myself, but in others, is how much vagal nerve stimulation can help your body. It's not just hocus pocus . . . this is all based on real science. Many studies have been done to prove how integral the vagus nerve is to so many functions in the body. When it's stimulated, we see major improvements in health, the reversal of unpleasant symptoms, and even the relief of many autoimmune diseases.

When we look at how well the vagus nerve works and how strong it is, we are looking at the vagal nerve tone, or how well your vagus nerve works. It's extremely important that your vagal tone is high if you want to stay healthy and be able to ward off diseases and stress. This can be done by stimulating or activating the vagus nerve. There are a number of ways to do just that, but first, you should understand more about the vagal tone.

Many factors can affect vagal tone and some people are more likely to have higher tone than others. For example, athletes and bodybuilders, as well as those who practice yoga, tend to have higher tone. Alcoholics, bedridden people, and those who don't exercise are at risk for lower vagal tone. It's also possible for you to have low vagal tone if your mother had low tone when pregnant with you. If she was stressed, angry, or anxious, it's likely that you were born with low vagal tone and may need to build it up.

Like bodybuilding, increasing your vagal tone means working out your vagus nerve. You need to keep activating it. How long should you do the activities given in this book? Fortunately, you don't need a long workout each day. You should aim for a total of 20 minutes or so per day. More is better, but as long as you are working on stimulating your vagus nerve daily, you are on the right track.

I suggest starting out by incorporating a few exercises into your daily routine. If you are rinsing your mouth, take the time to gargle a little longer. Showering? Sing or chant while you do so. It's fairly easy to add in a few little things and they all add up. The more you activate your vagus nerve, the more toned it will become and the more you'll notice yourself feeling better and stronger.

What is High Vagal Tone?

You want a high vagus nerve tone, since that means that your body is able to deal with stress very efficiently and can relax easily. It also means that your vagus nerve is better at regulating everything from digestion to blood sugar. Essentially, your nervous system is honed and ready to control everything to keep your body functioning at its best. When you have high vagal tone, you'll be more mentally resilient and your body will be much healthier.

It's amazing to see the difference in your body when your vagal tone is high. I couldn't believe how much difference there was once I had spent the time activating my vagus nerve. It does take some time to see results, but you go from being stressed and anxious all the time to being calm and relaxed even after a difficult day. That was something that changed gradually, but when I looked back, I could see the huge difference between the before and after. A lot of people would benefit from being able to recover from a bad time rapidly.

Higher vagal tone means that you will feel less stress and anxiety and will be able to move on quickly from unpleasant events. If you know someone who seems to brush off even awful things that happen to them, it may be that they just have high vagal tone. This means their fight or flight response doesn't kick in for every little thing and they are able to process everything calmly.

When your vagus nerve is properly toned, you'll also experience fewer headaches, and overall improved health. One of the biggest reasons I found to aim for high vagal tone was the fact that it reduces inflammation. Since inflammation is the major cause of many autoimmune diseases and other health issues, keeping it at bay is a major reason to stimulate your vagus nerve.

What is Low Vagal Tone?

If your vagal tone is too low, you'll find that you get sick far more often than usual. Your immune system will function poorly, since it is receiving little stimulation from the vagus nerve and that means any illness, bacteria, or virus can take hold quickly and easily. This is often seen in those who are under a lot of stress or who feel anxious most of the time. They will also tend to be sicker overall and will catch every passing cold or flu.

Low vagal tone is also associated with depression and feeling down. This is something that greatly affected me when I was dealing with the aftermath of vagus nerve damage. It was a chore to get out of bed every day. While this was partly to do with the pain I was managing, it was also the ongoing depression that crowded into my brain. Many people will tell you that depression is simply the lack of serotonin in the brain and while this is partially true, the vagus nerve manages the release of hormones and neurotransmitters, so it is responsible for the release of serotonin. If you have low vagal tone, you'll find that depression sets in easily.

Depression has also been linked to poor diet, which affects gut health. We already know that gut health can be a big factor in how well the vagus nerve works, so it's logical that there would be a connection between depression and poor gut health, as well. Remember, it's all connected and everything in your body affects the other parts.

When your vagal tone is low, you will also deal with higher stress levels and anxiety. I'll go more into these areas later on, but having dealt with them personally, I can tell you that they are some of the more unpleasant aspects of low vagal tone. It can become almost impossible to move past a simple, stressful event.

That's because your vagus nerve simply isn't able to work as well as it should, due to low tone.

If you do suffer from low vagal tone, there's still hope. Like a muscle, it can be improved by using it and stimulating it. The nervous system works best when it is being stimulated regularly and the vagus nerve is no different. In fact, there are plenty of ways to get your vagal tone up and it just requires knowing how to manipulate your nerves.

How to Measure Vagal Tone

Not sure if your vagus nerve tone is high or low? It is measured by looking at your heart rate. Everyone's heart speeds up slightly when they breathe in and becomes slightly slower when they breathe out. The difference between the two heart rates indicates just how toned your vagus nerve is. The bigger the difference, the higher your vagus tone is. If your body recovers quickly from just breathing, you know that you can recover quickly from other events, too. You should also check to see how fast your heart rate recovers from breathing in or out. High tone will result in a quick recovery, while low tone means the heart rate will lag slightly.

Your heart rate variation is the main way to test vagal tone, but there are other methods, as well. A simple way to check if your tone is high or low is to look at how you react to a stressful, yet harmless event. Do you dwell on it for the rest of the day and feel your anxiety spike every time you think about it? Or do you come up with a solution and move on to something else?

If you are able to calm your body automatically and move on with your day after a small, distressing event, your vagal tone is likely fairly high. However, if it haunts you for the rest of the day and maybe even overnight and into the next day, you may have low vagal tone.

Another method of checking is monitoring your breathing. It should be steady and not shallow or too fast. If you have the tendency to breathe too quickly and hyperventilate, you could have some issues with vagal tone. This is part of the reason you will find that breathing very deliberately and slowly will help you feel better.

Doctors may be able to check your vagal tone, as well, by measuring a combination of your breathing and heart rate. However, not all doctors are experienced with this method of diagnosing vagal tone and may not even be familiar with the term. It's best to find someone who is already experienced in the area and can help you figure out if your vagus nerve is functioning correctly.

No matter how toned your vagus nerve is, you can always benefit from stimulating it. Even if you aren't able to officially diagnose low vagal tone, you can always start activating the nerve and chances are, you'll see an improvement in your symptoms.

The Effects of Vagus Nerve Stimulation

Scientists have discovered that it is possible to stimulate the vagus nerve with an electronic implant that you activate with a magnetic strip. It's something that has been used successfully in both animals and humans. Those who have ongoing, chronic conditions, reported amazing results when they stimulated their vagus nerve multiple times daily.

People who could barely get out of bed in the morning due to chronic pain and stiffness were able to dance and swim and walk again. It sounds like a miracle, but it's really just the body doing what it is supposed to. When the nervous system is fully functional, you should be able to feel great and be able to do things without feeling too much pain. Unfortunately, what has become the norm is due to vagus nerve damage or poor vagal tone, but this is rarely diagnosed correctly.

Perhaps the most famous of the participants in the electronic stimulation test was Maria Vrind. Maria was a gymnast in her younger days, but rheumatoid arthritis had destroyed her body and made it difficult for her to walk, much less enjoy the activities she used to. She went through many different medications, including cancer treatments that lowered her immune system. Since rheumatoid arthritis is caused by inflammation, lowering the efficiency of the immune system can help give relief, but it has other consequences. The cancer drugs can cause a number of side effects, including nausea and since your immune system is lowered, you will get sick very frequently.

Maria took part in a trial where an electrical implant was installed in her body and connected to the vagus nerve endings in her throat. From there, she had to stimulate the nerve multiple times a day. To her surprise, it only took a few weeks before she was able to return to gymnastics. Others in the trial had similar experiences and those who didn't experience a miracle cure still saw results and chose to keep the implant after the trial ended.

Even minor changes to the vagus nerve can cause impressive results. There are more and more studies being done now to prove that vagal stimulation is useful in the treatment of more diseases. We are constantly learning more about the mysterious nervous system, including the vagus nerve.

Doctors can now offer a medical implant to help treat epilepsy, depression, and autoimmune diseases. The implant just stimulates the vagus nerve on a regular basis, causing it to reduce inflammation and release the necessary hormones to keep our bodies functioning at peak performance.

While Maria and others in the trial used a medical device to electronically send signals to their vagus nerve, it isn't necessary to implant something in your body to stimulate the vagus nerve. You can do it at home, without any special instruments. It simply requires commitment, since it can take some time to see the effects. You need to be able to see it through, even when you don't notice any immediate changes.

For those who are interested in improving vagal tone without having to resort to an implant and electronic stimulation, this book is packed with ways to stimulate the vagus nerve naturally. You have many options and they are all simple enough to do at home. Some require more effort than others, but they are all useful in boosting your overall health and reducing unpleasant symptoms.

Anxiety and Mindfulness

Reality is not always a suitable place for resting and healing. This is why many people go inside their minds to find solace and tranquility. Mindfulness can tap the source of your anxiety and stress, as well as relieve their symptoms.

In this chapter, you are going to learn how mindfulness meditation can minimize and diminish feelings of stress and anxiousness. You will also learn how to reduce the occurrence of panic attacks.

Social anxiety and panic attacks can affect a person's life. The feeling of being burned alive in public, while thinking that all eyes are upon you can cause irreparable trauma and emotional scars.

In such situations, you may feel palpitations, shaking, chest pain, and sweating. The feeling of being detached from your body or the world can cause loss of breath, nausea, and intense sensations of fear. Some even testify that they thought they were going crazy during a nervous breakdown or panic attack.

Practicing guided mindfulness meditation is an efficient way of managing feelings of anxiety and stress. Breathing techniques and simple meditation postures can be utilized as methods for relaxation and controlling and mitigating panic attacks.

Meditative practices can slow down racing thoughts, stop rumination, calm both your body and mind, and help you let go of negativity. Studies performed across geographical borders, gender, and age groups have exhibited the power of the practice to the world.

For instance, the 2015 clinical study conducted in Harvard showed a drop in the number of stressed and anxious nursing students. The participants were instructed to practice mindfulness meditation breathing techniques. In 2019, similar findings were revealed. The participants, however, in the 2nd study were US adolescents who were diagnosed with anxiety.

People with anxiety, whether a child, a teenager, an adult, or an elderly, tend to worry about the future and the past. Past events make them hide behind their walls, and the unknown future makes their stomach queasy. Their fear, or their past experiences hinder them from living their life to the fullest.

By focusing on the present moment, through mindfulness meditation, you can heal and slowly break your protective shell.

In most cases, anxiety stems from too much stress. When you have too many problems on your plate, you will start to worry and become frustrated. Later on, you'll feel stressed out. Then, this is when negative thoughts, anxiety, and depression may start to hug your mind.

If you're always looking behind your shoulders and the feeling of being "alert" becomes background noise, it's time to do something with your anxiety. With mindfulness meditation, you will say goodbye to panic attacks and nights of loneliness and fear.

In 3-Steps, Calm Your Mind and Stop That Panic Attack!

You are going to first learn the quick methods you can use outside the safety of your home. Later on, the proper posture, forms, and techniques will be discussed. You can get started now!

1. Focus your attention to the present moment

Remember that mindfulness is a psychological process. So you can direct or will your mind to practice it. All you have to do for the first step is to bring your attention to experiences that are occurring in the present time. Do not cloud your mind with judgment or other thoughts. Just focus on this task. The ultimate goal of this simple exercise is to make yourself a container for all of the sensations present in your body. Envision your sensations and feelings in a widescreen. Imagine that you can watch them inside you and that they can pass you.

2. Breathing

Once you have that big screen established, avert your mind and senses away from it for a while. Instead, focus on your breathing. Narrow your focus on inhaling and exhaling in a specific region of your body. For example, only think and feel the sensations of breathing through your nostrils or the subtle rise and fall of your belly. Concentrate your focus there.

3. Be aware of your body.

After step 2, you must become attentive with your other body sensations. Close your eyes. Feel the weight of your body against the mat/chair or hear the slow humming sound of the air conditioner. Does the air make your hair stood on ends or is it too hot for you? What do your 5 senses feel? You must be able to answer these questions within your mind.

When you focus on the present or your physical experiences, you stop overthinking. You prevent rumination from culminating. Rumination is closely related to worry. Both are associated with negative emotional states, such as anxiety.

Based on some research, anxiety diminishes when you give yourself some space from what you're experiencing. This includes trying to detach yourself from the stressors of your life, but not in a literal sense. This doesn't mean that you should evade or run away from your problems.

Rather, it's best to stop thinking about them because worrying and overthinking doesn't help. They only worsen the situation. Focus your attention on other things, such as the rustling of the leaves, the passing of the clouds, or the sensations around you. Bring your consciousness to the present, not to the past or future, so that you can have a sound mind that can solve problems and formulate solutions.

How Mindfulness Meditation Relieves Anxious Feelings

Desiring to look for an emotional pillar in which you can rest your weary soul is never easy unless you truly trust someone with your life. Your family, including your parents, siblings, or spouse, could be your major emotional support.

In times of need, you call them, and you seek their touch. You want to curl your fingers between the palms of your spouse, just to ease that fear ebbing in your stomach. Anxiety has numerous effects, and it also has a variety of causes.

Not everyone with anxiety feels cautious or is a worrywart all the time. Sometimes, they only feel anxious when specific stimuli trigger feelings of anxiousness and dread. These feelings can cause panic attacks, stress, extreme fear, and insomnia.

When your emotional support isn't there, what will you do? Will you curl into a ball and wait for the sun to rise? What if you can't sleep? Will you resort to pills or mutilation? Never hurt yourself because of your condition. Don't make things worse than they already are.

It's also not wise to drop everything and just run away. Sure, that's the shortest route, but remember that your actions today affect your future. Not only does anxiety hinders you from doing things, but it can also ruin your life.

Studies have revealed that guided mindfulness meditation helps in reducing the symptoms of depression and anxiety. By becoming aware of your mental and physical state in the present moment, you can come up with adaptive reactions to social and difficult situations.

Mindfulness meditation works in various ways, but overall, it promotes the uncovering, understanding, and acceptance of emotions, whether positive or negative.

To practice mindfulness, you must first be more reflective than reactive. Don't alter your behavior or performance, just because someone is watching you. You must exhibit nonjudgemental awareness of the present experiences, including the environment, bodily states, thoughts, and sensations.

Guided mindfulness meditation enables you to detach yourself from your feelings and thoughts without being able to label them as bad or good. This prevents rumination and overthinking. It also counteracts worrying.

Blaming yourself for your past actions, worrying about your future, and daydreaming are maladaptive thinking processes, in general. These thought patterns are referred to as cognitive distortions.

They make you perceive reality inaccurately, and they induce depression and anxiety. As stated by Aaron T. Beck, a negative outlook of reality diminishes one's self-esteem and causes emotional dysfunction. Your willpower weakens, and you lose the ability to make a sound judgment.

Negative thought patterns create negative emotions. During difficult situations, distorted thoughts contribute to the perpetuation of an anxious or depressive mental state.

It is vital as a human being to learn from past mistakes and to plan for one's future. Nevertheless, when one spends too much time outside the present, one can become anxious or depressed.

Mindfulness encourages positive responses to stress through awareness of present experiences. Instinctive or reactive responses are often not governed by rational thinking. By being aware of your mental and physical state, you can come up with adaptive reactions to dire situations.

Awareness is the key to controlling panic attacks and stopping mental breakdowns. For this to happen, you must be able to identify, experience, and process your emotions.

Here's a simple meditation exercise for combating negative thoughts.

When you start to practice mindfulness, it is advised to do so in a distraction-free and quiet area. The time for meditation will depend on you and your needs. For example, if you want to reduce morning anxiety, begin your day with a meditation.

This sets a positive and clear tone for the whole day. If you want to relieve tension and fatigue, meditate after dinner. It also helps you have a good night's sleep, enabling you to sleep like a log.

a)   To begin meditating, reserve at least 10 minutes of your time. Day by day, you can increase the length of time.

b)   Next, sit down in a comfortable position. Start meditating with a breathing technique or just exhale and inhale slowly and deeply.

c)   By this time, you should start noticing your thoughts. Permit ideas to enter your mind. At this stage, don't be judgemental about yourself. You should just let the thoughts flow.

d)   Remain in the present. If negative ideas arise, or you recall something embarrassing, try your best to let those thoughts pass, like how vehicles pass the protagonist in a movie.

e)   Again, focus on your breathing. When the time is up, take a few more deep breaths and open your eyes.

Other than calming yourself, mindfulness meditation also makes you more open-minded. It encourages you to see situations or issues from multiple perspectives.

For instance, if your loved one seems angry at you for no apparent reason, you may blame yourself and begin to worry that you have done something wrong again. You would feel hurt and dejected.

However, if you can detach yourself from your usual response, you will be able to remember that your spouse has a taxing job. He or she could have had a hard time at work. Perhaps, your partner snapped at you because he or she is stressed out too.

New interpretations can alleviate negative feelings and reduce worrying. Practicing mindfulness enhances body awareness, self-perception, and focused attention.

What Are They? Are They Important?

1. Body Awareness

Body awareness is the feeling that you have for your body. It is the understanding of the different parts that make up your body. This includes their location, sensations, and function. Body awareness also includes the emotional state of a person. Being aware of them is required in regulating your emotions.

2. Focused Attention

Focused attention is a cognitive skill. It is important in learning and problem-solving processes. Your brain can concentrate its awareness on a particular stimulus for any period.

Neuroimaging research has revealed that mindfulness meditations encourage the use of the ACC or anterior cingulate cortex. The ACC is a region in your brain involved in attention and executive function.

By controlling your brain's focus, it will be easier for you to concentrate on a single task. You shouldn't let your mind focused on worry or other similar distractions.

3. Self-perception

The self-perception theory explains that people determine their preferences and attitudes by perceiving their behavior or by knowing oneself. They also tend to copy the behavior, virtues, look, and attitude of people they admire.

Mindfulness meditation can also change your self-image. The "self" or your "ego" isn't static and permanent. Buddhist psychologists argue that it is composed of present mental events, including dreams, realizations, feelings, and decisions. Studies have shown that 1 month of guided mindfulness meditation improves one's self-acceptance and self-esteem.

As stated by Shepard, self-acceptance is a person's happiness or satisfaction with oneself. It is necessary for your mental health and for producing positive thoughts. It involves awareness of one's weaknesses and strengths and self-understanding.

4. Physical health

It is evident that mindfulness meditation diminishes stress. It hinders the production of cortisol, the stress hormone. It lowers cortisol levels in your bloodstream. Hence, practicing mindfulness decreases the risk of diseases caused by stress, which includes migraine, peptic ulcer, and psychiatric disorders.

Honestly, there are no tenets or strict regimen required for practicing this discipline. All it requires are concentration and the focus on the present moment. You can actually apply mindfulness to any activity.

For instance, you can either eat mindlessly or savor every bite by tasting the flavors and feeling their texture with your tongue. Taking your time to enjoy your food by tasting it is better than mindlessly gobbling down your meal.

Many modern and traditional disciplines include mindfulness practices in their tenets. This includes zen, yoga, and tai chi. Many styles exist for the practice and some are designed for particular conditions, such as anxiety and mood disorders.

As you become a more mindful person, you will see that you'll feel more satisfied, happier, and centered than before. And, the markers for your anxiety will diminish. Its somatic symptoms, including panic attacks and extreme dread, will go away as well.

To be mindful right now, be aware of your breathing for several minutes. Feel the rise and fall of your chest and concentrate on the sensations produced by your breathing. Feel the air around you, or be conscious of your breathing. What do you feel when you exhale and inhale? What's the taste of the air around you?

As you perform this simple exercise, do find the answer to those questions. If you start to think of other things, just simply pull your attention back to breathing and remember to concentrate on the present. With this, you will be able to feel how good it is to be alive.

Some practitioners even perform mindfulness exercises outside the security of their homes. Being surrounded by nature helps in relieving stress and releasing anxiety. For beginners, you should practice meditation at home first, especially if you have social anxiety.

Place a bushy or tall potted plant near your exercise area. When you perform breathing exercises, you should face the plant so that you can smell its natural scent. You may add two or more potted plants. This makes it feel less cramp for you, and it recreates a sort of natural setting inside your home.

The 3 Minutes Breathing Space

This simple exercise is utilized in MBCT programs and Cognitive Behavior Therapies. It helps people get unstuck and move forward with their lives, even after embarrassing breakdowns.

While performing this mindfulness practice, refrain from evaluating and choosing your thoughts. Instead, you have to become aware of them and your breathing. The previous exercises made you concentrate on one part of your body.

Contrastingly, the 3 minutes breathing space will make you expand your senses. As a beginner, you will only be required to focus on your breathing. But you have to be mindful of the effect of respiration on various areas of your body. Feel the sensations it creates and its effects on your body as a whole.

Does that sound too complicated? Well, don't fret because it is very easy to practice. It only involves 3 simple steps.

a)	Firstly, look for a comfortable area wherein you can't be disturbed by anyone. And if possible, turn off your cellphone and laptop. There must be no distractions. Next, notice the thoughts inside your head, and don't change the things you're observing.

b)	The second step involves focusing on your breathing. Sit in a covered flat surface and sit up straight. Once you are settled, concentrate on your intake and expelling of air. Be aware of the rise and fall of your chest and abdomen. Feel the air as it enters and escapes your nostrils. What do you smell? Do you hear your breathing?

c)	Third, you have to expand your senses. You should still focus on your breathing, but all the while, you must be aware of the other sensations your body is feeling. Other noise or disturbances are unnecessary. Are your legs cramping? Do you feel hot or cold? Be aware and focus on those sensations as well.

The goal of this exercise is to establish awareness for body sensations and to emphasize shifting of attention and moving on from one focus to another. Accordingly, you should only linger for a minute in each step. The 3MBS exercise prepares you for other mindfulness practices, and it encourages "moving of attention."

The exercise can help you get unstuck from automatic routines. It also provides you space wherein you can get a breather from stress or taxing tasks.

Time and time again, mindfulness has been proven to improve symptoms of anxiety, PTSD, and depression. Compared to other meditative practices, mindfulness is straightforward and has no hard to follow prerequisites.

You have now been acquainted to the easiest and most efficient mindfulness practices. You can use them, whenever you're having a hard time or a sudden panic attack.

In public, it can be hard to deal with panic attacks. The 3 minutes breathing space can help you gain control of your mind and your body. Often, nervous breakdown stems from extreme stress or fear.

You have to conquer them in order for you to move forward. Picture your triggers in a big screen. Treat them as if they are just an element of a movie. By doing so, you can see them in a different light.

While calming yourself with breathing techniques, study the stimuli, and eventually, you will learn to accept them.

Conclusion

Thank you, dear reader, for taking the time to read through this book and learn of anxiety and how to overcome the challenges that the disorder causes. Throughout the book, we have attempted to give details on how you can manage the situation, considering that mental health issues rarely have a permanent cure as of the current medical situation. However, you can mitigate the effects of the illness. Even when we do not know of anyone who is mentally ill, chances are, we have suffered from mental breakdowns as a result of many factors shaped by the ups and downs of life. We have been anxious and depressed at some points in our lives.

Your mindset is often the beginning of every other thing that you do. So, we gave you details on how you can improve your mindset to reduce the effects of anxiety.

We then gave you a self-esteem booster in Anxiety chews away your confidence in ways that you may not even be aware of. One time, you are happy and outgoing. The next minute, you are crushing under the weight of panic attacks. You lose confidence in your abilities and think that you are not important. Well, you are, and as we have seen in you need to keep your head high.

We have then looked in detail about what anxiety is and how it can be triggered. While there are many triggers, one common thing about fear is that it often thrives and grows in uncertainty.

We have then looked at the types of anxiety, among the general anxiety disorder, where someone spends days on end worrying about various different things; social anxiety, where someone gets really disturbed in social situations; and post-traumatic stress disorder, which is often the result of a haunting and life-altering event such as an accident or violence among others. All these different anxiety disorders will often have their remedies, but you can still mitigate them when you recognize consistent patterns among them all.

Here, we trust you took in how you can reconnect with nature to find relaxation, practicing gratitude, which will improve your view of the world, eating healthy, and of course, keeping a journal, which you can use to mark important happenings in your new life to map your progress.

What is the essence of your being? This will help you know yourself so that you do not fall back into the pitfalls of being anxious and restless. You will understand what made you anxious and why, and then make the moves to improve how you react to different stimuli.

Our emotions are vital components of who we are. It is through them that we understand others better and the world in general. Thus, getting in touch with your emotions will give you an insight into how they shape your anxiety; therefore, how you can stop them from making things worse. Emotions, after all, are distinctly human as far as we know, and so, to understand them will be to understand humanity.

Then, in een, we gave you tips on how to identify your potential, both as you recover and as you begin to focus more on your career. Reaching your potential is one of the major signs that you are moving forward. To get here, you have overcome the crippling effects of your anxiety and are, therefore, looking to live your life beyond your anxiety. You want more than just to be limited to your anxieties.

After all, you are a better person. You need better, fresher goals.

So, we hope that you have found the lessons in this book useful and informative. Please anyone with anxiety about it.

Thank you once more.